AF508471

Evolving to Extinction

An [un]serious condemnation of our
uniquely human behavior

Brian Webster

Copyright © 2026 by Empathy Echoes LLC

All rights reserved

First Edition

Printed in the United States of America

ISBNs:

979-8-9956578-2-8 hardcover

979-8-9956578-0-4 paperback

979-8-9956578-1-1 ebook

979-8-9956578-3-5 audiobook

www.brainsbri.com

@brainsbri

Design by Scott Luttmann

Illustration by Lucky Sok

For Us

Hello fellow humans!

Thank you for opening this book. Maybe you bought it, maybe it was a gift from a friend, or maybe you randomly found it somewhere. Perhaps you unwillingly found yourself in possession of a copy to appease a crazy relative who relentlessly forced their copy on you.

Either way, I am grateful that you are reading these words.

I am publishing physical copies of this book in the most resource-efficient way possible, and I have a crazy idea to further reduce our resource usage while still spreading this message. Make your mark in the book and pass it along to another reader.

Yes, go ahead and write in the book. Yes, give it away.

There is plenty of white space on each page, a consequence of my writing style that conveniently opens the door for leaving a simple Date and General Location tag, or whatever mark you wish, near a favorite passage or other random location.

Get creative with it! Whatever works to connect with your fellow readers. If you're on the socials, post a pic so we can collectively experience the journey of each copy.

Let's all have a good laugh at ourselves. Together.

Welcome

Opening remarks

How the hell are we still here?

A deceptively simple question that actually lacks an obvious answer. What a feat, though, our uninterrupted reign on this beautiful rock of ours.

We did it. Great job, everybody!

The fact that we somehow still exist as a species is our greatest collective achievement. Forget the dizzying array of impressive innovations differentiating us from our fellow earthly inhabitants:

- If you live in the civilized world, you would probably die without your smartphone.

- Video games keep us busy in our youth, and sometimes into adulthood — much to the dismay of our spouse and kids.

- Not having to hunt for meals is a plus.

- Air travel is pretty sweet.

- AI can do most of our desk work now, and it incessantly starts each response with a bit of flattery to keep us hooked.

- Have you seen all the latest advancements in window treatments?

- How about that wheel, and all those other simple machines?

- Not dying from simple infections has been lovely.

We are the overachievers of the species world who are still managing to run the earth show.

First place, y'all! We persevered and climbed to the top.

Against all odds. Against all species — or so we think.

Given all the other living beings roaming the earth, have you ever once wondered how we as a species claimed the throne?

What makes us so unique?

Or do we all just take our position for granted, accepting it as fate or divine will because it is just the way it has always been?

Are there more pragmatic reasons for our success, such as the standard go-to argument citing our superior intellect and reasoning abilities? Perhaps it's our advanced communication skills that most of us have mastered.

Emphasis on *most*.

We could also credit our insatiable ambition and robotic productivity that we feverishly deploy in defense of our overachiever crown.

Then we have those unique anatomical attributes that we typically invoke, like our opposable thumbs.

That's always a fan favorite.

One entertaining novel I read recently — a work of fiction, as a reminder — even suggested that our complex shoulder joints led to our rise because we could throw a spear. I suppose hunting from a distance is more sensible than wrestling a mammoth.

With all this *Homo sapiens* awesomeness running rampant, I am left wondering how we haven't yet disappeared off the face of the planet.

It feels like we are close, though.

One too many disgruntled, senile, predominantly male world leaders keep their shaky fingers hovering over too many big red nuclear buttons for my personal comfort level right now.

Ignoring for the moment the threat of a nuclear apocalypse, and in spite of our amazing success on this *species dominance* game show where we inexplicably fail to realize we are the only participant, our days are numbered due to our unique human behavior on this planet. Distinct behaviors disguised as societal norms that have us on a tortoise-paced crash course with our own demise.

We may avoid spontaneous eradication in the near-term, but our daily choices ever so slightly jeopardize our long-term existence in a less perceptible way.

In perhaps the greatest irony in the history of all that is ironic, we are incrementally evolving our way to extinction.

Everything we have ever engineered in the course of our existence has made our lives easier, consequently reducing our resilience in the natural world as we frolic around in a customized artificial playground that we superimposed on the planet, ignorantly and gleefully swinging on the monkey bars as the rest of our fellow species friends watch the world burn.

We will without question endure whatever happens in the *very near* future. We will power through. We always do, at least for now, and that'll presumably buy us another century or so.

Jumping to the other end of the timeline, the *way too distant* future, there is that not-so-looming threat of our sun going supernova in a few billion years.

I present my proposed bookends for the end of humanity: anywhere between 2125 and the year 5,000,002,125. We as a species will assuredly die off somewhere within this extremely specific and totally narrow range.

Since my predictive powers are clearly on point and amazingly precise right now, I also took the liberty of printing tonight's winning lottery numbers in the back of this book.

You're welcome.

Since a *five-billion*-year range is without a doubt useless, my uninformed and uneducated guess would be that we are looking at between multiple millennia, but not quite eons, until we carve the *Homo sapiens* tombstone.

That internet thingy says *myriad* would work here if we accept its classical definition of 10,000, so let's have some fun and run with that. *Myriad millennia* left on our species clock, which equates to somewhere around the year 10,002,025 or so?

Mark your calendars, everyone!

If there is any validity at all to my argument, we are *relatively* close to the end of the road.

Definitely not our problem, right? That's too far off in the future for us to truly care. Who could possibly fathom that length of time anyway? No one is walking around in 2025 asking what their friends will be doing in the year 23,249.

We'll all be dead.

Why would that year even cross our minds when we are concerned with present-day matters like paying our bills this month, or getting our kids to all their activities this week. Half of us don't even know what the hell to make for dinner, with the other half wondering if there will even be dinner on the table tonight.

But while our decisions today appear to have no impact on that distant timeframe, every decision we make today can have profound impacts millennia from now. The argument that we have no long-lasting impact appears valid at our current zoom level, but right now our faces are simply too close to the ruler to notice the big picture.

What does *a long time* mean to you? A decade? Half a century? Maybe a millennium?

Our discussion dwarfs those timeframes, and it is this shortsightedness that convinces us our daily actions could never veer us off course on this ship our species finds itself on right now.

If we're hypothetically sailing to a destination a kilometer away using a compass as our guide, a one-degree course error that we unknowingly maintain throughout the entire journey still puts us pretty close to our final destination. It wouldn't be perfect, but we would get there.

Let's exaggerate and say our destination is now 225 million kilometers away, and we unknowingly maintain the same consistent one-degree course error on our journey. We would miss our target by quite a bit, and we may very well end up in a different solar system.

I also just not-so-subtly transitioned from sea to space. Buckle up, I'm one of those humans still working on their communication skills.

At any rate, the angle between our true course and errant course is the same miniscule magnitude in both scenarios, but the change in distance between the original target and the actual arrival point grows significantly the farther out we travel.

Enough words. I am trying out this whole writing thing, but I'm still a visual person.

Connecting our hypothetical travel analogy to our very real behavior, our seemingly trivial actions today may not exhibit much impact tomorrow or a year from now, but their collective and continued occurrence can wreak havoc down the road.

Irrelevant to our immediate offspring, but a looming catastrophe for our great^{500}-grand kids and beyond.

The $^{"500"}$ is just an exponent to save space and prevent any potential eye strain induced by repetitively reading the word 'great' across an entire page. Don't go looking for a long list of footnotes.

It's not all doom and gloom, though. We don't need to go back to the stone age, even though I might go that route.

While I'm perfectly content typing these words in a comfortable workspace sipping a cappuccino and writing on a battery-powered device while wirelessly connected to the internet, there is a certain allure to the Walden-style, off-grid 'cabin in the woods' setup.

Not that horror movie 'cabin in the woods' craziness, but more like a sweet little 'cottage in the forest' vibe.

You do you, though. We are all adults, I think. At least according to age, we meet that criterion and can make our own choices.

If it's all good, though, then why is this book in your hands?

After a few random life observations, a quarter-life reset (not a crisis), and the onset of a mid-life break (also not a crisis), I thought it would be entertaining to acknowledge a few uniquely human behaviors that didn't quite make our species highlight reel.

Programmed actions and subconscious learned behaviors that go unnoticed by us and set us apart from every other species on the planet.

Actions that simultaneously and paradoxically point us in the direction of near-term advancement and long-term extinction.

The little things we do every day that appear to cause nothing now but collectively lead to substantial long-term impacts down the road.

The natural world is perplexed by us, and our fellow planetary inhabitants are presumably left wondering when we will get the hint. In a nature documentary-style role reversal, the rest of our fellow species are grabbing their version of popcorn, plopping themselves onto their version of a couch, and sitting back to watch this shit show unfold, wondering if the planetary apex species actually pulls this one off.

It's a bold strategy, our approach to existing on this planet, and we'll see how it plays out.

So have a laugh, shed a tear, and whatever you're drinking, pour one out for humanity, because we are on a million-year crash course with [maybe] becoming the first species to cause their own extinction.

What's a book without a thesis?

But first some boring administrative garbage to further set the stage for our riveting conversation.

Thesis time! Remember those?

I hate them too, but without one my mind would forever wander and I would never finish writing. You would have a senseless mash-up of random insults and whiny complaints in your hands right now and you would all find a way to give this thing negative stars on review sites.

Apparently, writers seamlessly integrate said thesis into the introductory material, but I am leaving it as a stand-alone statement for emphasis. Apologies to my middle school English teachers for going off-script. Here you go:

Our continuous isolation from the biosphere and our significant imbalance with nature will eventually lead us to self-extinction. As we partition ourselves from the rest of the system, we refuse to acknowledge the detrimental effects of our actions out of view beyond our immediate surroundings. We are pushing out of balance with the natural world because we have a false sense of abundance, we are obsessed with comfort, and contentment continues to elude us.

That was a bit academic. How about we translate that really quickly:

We are committing species suicide by behaving in unnatural ways compared to every other species on this planet. We isolate ourselves from the natural world, wholly convinced that we can out-engineer the natural systems that have existed on this planet since the dawn of fucking time, and we suffer from a serious case of denial as we operate under the assumption that we can completely remake the face of the earth like a game and experience absolutely zero negative consequences.

Before tossing this book in the trash, remember that you are reading an unserious assessment of our societal choices. A casual exploration of human action combined with a sprinkle of comic relief that we'll close out with an unconvincingly-inflated sense of hope.

A thesis at its core is really just an opinion of sorts, and who am I anyway? I am certainly no expert.

I am merely proposing that we are driving our species off a cliff, but the cliff is well beyond the horizon line, we are ignorantly approaching it at a snail's pace, and all we have to do at this moment right now to avoid the catastrophe we don't see coming is the equivalent of tilting our head a few degrees in a different direction.

Our responsibility is minimal, your cocktail party next week can still happen, and there is conveniently no pressure on me to support my argument since I'll be long gone before anyone can pass final judgment on this theory.

Send all complaints to my progeny.

Stupid questions, insightful answers

I like questions.

I *love* stupid questions.

You have already seen a few of them, and I will continue to ask them throughout this book.

We give stupid questions too little attention and thought. We immediately dismiss them, but that is a trained reaction meant to prevent deeper contemplation about certain cultural norms ingrained in us since birth.

Thinking about these stupid questions helps us challenge that programmed thinking, which is why I opened the book with one:

"How the hell are we still here?"

Curious minds enjoy answering stupid questions, while fearful minds avoid them. Frightened minds confronted with that opening question would default to justifications like: "Duh, why wouldn't we be?", "Where would we go?", and "We're the best!" because these individuals outright reject the mere thought of human inferiority.

We think very highly of ourselves if you haven't noticed.

It is uncomfortable at first, as the invisible arbiters of our culture and society — the mystical and proverbial 'they' that we all fear — pass judgment on us for attempting to dissect a question that has always been off-limits for additional analysis.

Stupid questions unlock amazing new perspectives. They force us to pause and think through our assumptions, and they open up a part of our brains otherwise guarded by our systematic, ordered, process-driven world.

If you stumble across any preposterous questions as you read this book, push through your initial desire to call me an idiot, read them, think about them, and truly answer them.

While I certainly qualify as an idiot by most measures, I can assure you that I put these questions where they are for a reason.

Get your metric on...

In honor of the individual I saw at the fair last summer wearing a sleeveless black t-shirt proudly depicting a bald eagle, a flag, and fancy text that said, "WTF is a kilogram?", I will unapologetically use the metric system throughout this book.

Meters and liters and Celsius, oh my.

You will also see times in 24-hour format, because there are 24 hours in a day and each hour should have a distinct designation. If you see a time you don't recognize, just subtract 12 and you'll survive.

To my American audience, and hopefully one day my Liberian and Burmese readers, I'm sorry to say that we are skipping the arbitrary measurement system based on some dead dude's foot.

...but not your metrics

I am not including any significant supporting data in this book.

Precise numbers.

Detailed graphs.

Equations.

Calculations.

Statistics.

Metrics and measures.

This book is intentionally devoid of all that fun stuff.

Why?

Well, for starters, I refuse to change the clever little chapter title transition I already came up with — 'Get your metrics on...not your metrics' — so I'm sticking with it.

I'm also lazy and don't feel like doing any more work than necessary, especially since I'm just sharing my opinion.

Lastly, I'm self-publishing, so I can do whatever the hell I want.

We are mildly obsessed with this data stuff that can tell whatever story we want with it. Data-based insights, data acquisition, data science, data analytics, and data-based decision making, with data centers galore to support it all. Two people can apply their own criteria to the same data set and tell different, sometimes contradictory stories.

Data is also a great way to feel confident — "The data says so!" — while somehow also providing a scapegoat if it all goes wrong — "It's the data's fault that reality didn't align with our expectations!" — so I'm removing that safety blanket.

We suffer from data overload, and this isn't a book that requires such in-depth technical analysis. After a life of data, I'm running on all feels with this one, sparing myself the painful effort of gathering data and resorting to scolding everyone like the minimalist hermit that I am.

This book is nothing more than my perspective that I feel compelled to share, presented in a way that hopefully causes at least one of you to lol or lmao or rofl at least once.

A conceptual view of the world from my eyes.

No data required.

Enjoy the ride

Alright, let's have some fun!

Don't take things so seriously.

Or do.

Your choice!

I don't know what I'm talking about, remember? I am no more than an out of touch luddite here bringing you an unpopular view of our amazingness, so let's get started!

Our Planet as a System

This broken system

Yes. If there is one thing we can agree on, it's that the system is broken.

We've all said it, we all seem to know it, but can we actually explain what that 'system' *is,* the one we so liberally bitch about?

Most cannot, so before I jump into making fun of us as a species we must drudge through the monotony a little bit more to ensure we can properly visualize the system in which we all live.

Pretend you are looking at the side of the earth, and using your imaginary marker, circle the parts of the ground and atmosphere where life naturally exists, both above and below the surface. You just found earth's biosphere.

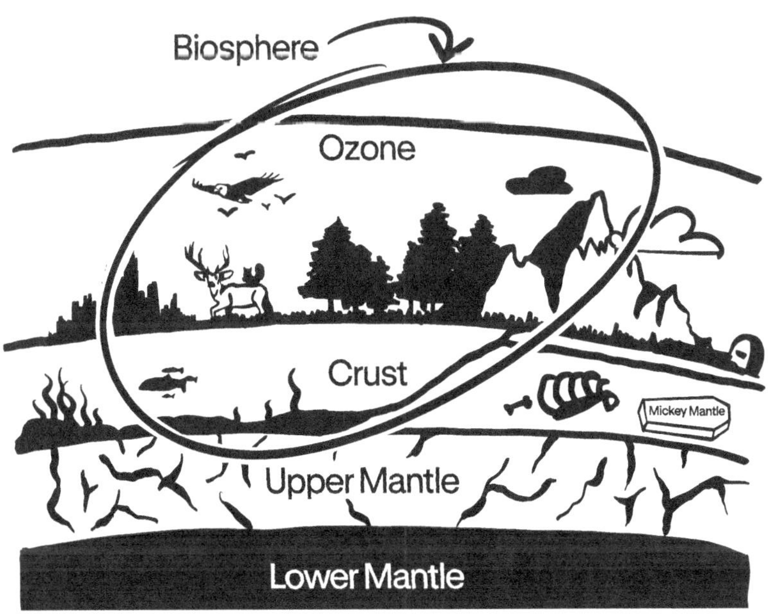

The biosphere is a *system*: basically, a set of things working together. You are familiar with systems, since you hear the word often enough:

Sound system.

Legal system.

Gaming system.

Transportation system.

Financial system.

HVAC system.

Education system.

Electrical system.

Infotainment system.

Metric system.

Economic system.

IT system.

And the list goes on. I couldn't possibly name them all.

Systems are everywhere, and countless deeply intertwined subsystems can exist within a larger system.

When you start diving into the subsystem stuff, you quickly see that a single automobile has a dozen or so subsystems, like those electrical and infotainment systems I just mentioned. There are also ten or so subsystems in a residential home, including that HVAC subsystem, and a different electrical subsystem than the one in your car.

There are a dozen or so subsystems in the human body. Hell, try figuring out the systems at work in the human brain alone with all those neurons, dendrites, and synapses up there.

Work through this painful exercise long enough and you'll see the list of individual systems, if written out, would probably wrap around the equator. They are numerous, annoyingly complicated, and downright confusing, and depending on where we draw the line, something could be a system, a subsystem, or both.

I listed *infotainment*, *HVAC*, and *electrical* systems as both systems and subsystems in the span of two pages, and I used the term *electrical* for two systems that differ based on context.

Having fun yet?

These systems are the gears that drive this world, and their complex interactions are nearly impossible to grasp, further complicating our ability to see how the world truly works. Our standard quantification approach with math and numbers doesn't cut it, no matter how hard we try.

We think we understand, but who are we kidding? We're making this shit up as we go.

To avoid further complications, we'll stay out of the earth's core, and we'll also avoid space and the solar system for this book and use the biosphere as our top-level system.

As we begin descending into the biosphere a bit we find a wide array of subsystems, passing by biomes for now and getting right to *ecosystems*. You know those, too, and don't bother trying to count them all either. Texas alone probably has about a dozen.

But there is also an unnatural subsystem taking root among all those ecosystems, an entity introduced by humans that actually includes every system I listed to start this chapter.

Or is it every subsystem?

See, I can't even keep it straight, so we'll just say the biosphere is our system, and everything else we discuss within is just a subsystem.

The biosphere is pretty resilient, but it's also pretty pissed right now.

Possibly.

I'm no earth-whisperer, but it seems the natural world is slowly rejecting this artificial transplant of ours.

Our humanity bubble

Our bodies are physically present on this planet, but we exist within a dream world. Welcome to our *humanity bubble*, that bad transplant the earth is subtly fighting.

Also welcome to the biggest pain in the ass of this entire book.

This concept plays a key part in our discussion, so I will do my best with this explanation. We'll get through it together, so please bear with me as I present one way to visualize our current living situation.

We debate an impending virtual reality takeover involving computers, headsets, and VR goggles, but we are already living in a fake environment that we superimposed on this earth.

The reality we know, this *humanity bubble* of ours, is not real.

From a human perspective it is normal, but from a natural standpoint it is a complete fabrication that goes against how every other living organism on this planet operates.

Our little world is a sanitary world.

Excessively hygienic.

Squeaky-clean and lemony-fresh.

It is shielded from the elements.

Dry and comfortable.

Temperature controlled.

Humidity controlled.

Perpetually well-lit.

Safe.

Tame.

Well-provisioned.

It has plenty of distractions for us, and includes more reality TV shows than any species could ever need. A custom-made, picture-perfect, synthetic ecosystem for most of humanity and our domesticated animal friends.

It is ours. It is perfect. You love it, and I love it, too.

I am personally relieved that I don't have to protect my children from bobcats and wolves. My clothing conveniently prevents mosquito bites as I write outside on a beautiful summer evening. I've also never gone more than a day without food or water.

This bubble of ours seems like a sweet deal, and while it is custom-designed to support our comfort and survival, we are so entranced by its splendor that we are either incapable or unwilling to see it as a species life support that forcibly keeps our highly intelligent but comparatively weak species at the top.

In this *humanity bubble* we go about our lives, but fail to truly live a natural life.

Now, calling our human world a bubble may not be the best analogy, since there isn't a single continuous circle demarcating 'our part' of the planet from nature. This bubble has a bit more of a 3-D chess vibe in terms of complexity, and is much more intertwined than that simple circle we made around the biosphere earlier. Think of the world as a bunch of mini-bubbles, or even better, a few individual pixels on a TV or monitor that form the image you see on the screen.

Similar to a mosaic: a single, large image composed of thousands of tiny images.

We can think of the planet in the same way but we just need to add some depth, so let's first pretend we're looking straight down at the entire map of earth on that TV screen with millions of tiny little pixels. The *size* of the pixels we see is irrelevant. Square meters, square millimeters. Feel free to pick your [metric] unit of choice. Now imagine we tilt our heads slightly and look at the map again from an angle, but instead of seeing square, 2-D pixels we now see stacks of 3-D cubes above and below the plane of the TV screen.

The omniscient internet just informed me that I could use the term *voxels* here to refer to these cubes, but this whole thing is confusing enough so we're sticking with *cube*.

The TV screen itself serves as the earth's surface, the boundary between the air and the land or sea that we'll assume is at a uniform level for this illustration. Grab your beach chairs, everyone, we're all hanging at sea level today!

The cubes extending *above* the TV capture the livable air space. The cubes extending *below* the TV represent subterranean earth or water.

Good so far?

I am the creator of this ridiculous analogy and I'm lost, so let's again defer to another visual.

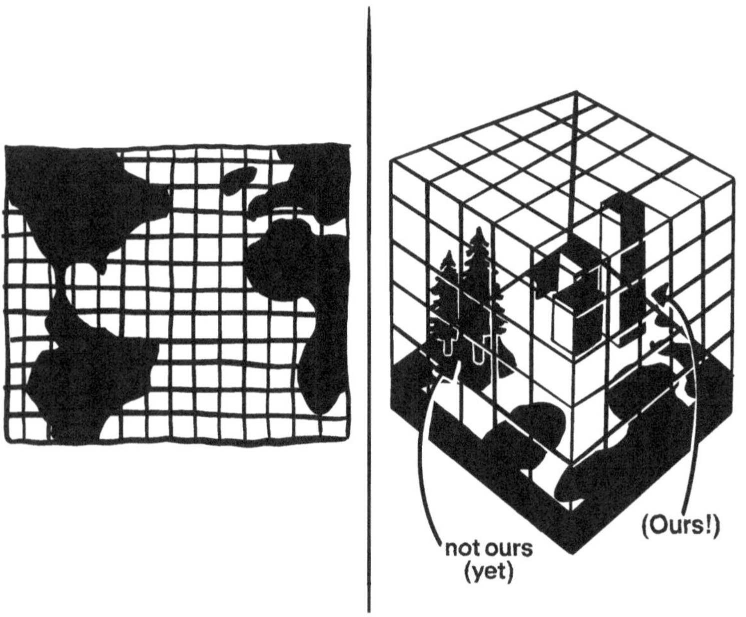

A cubic representation of the entire biosphere where each small cube is either in our *humanity bubble*, or part of the natural world.

That's right, my analogy for a bubble has corners.

They can't all be winners. I also figure that anyone who has ever played that crazy world-building game with different colored cubes and a tasty chicken made with lava could easily relate.

There will also be no quantum computing "It can be a 1 and a 0 at the same time!" nonsense here in regard to the status of each cube. It's straight classical computing for us. Either a 1 or 0 in the sense that a cube can be either in the *humanity bubble* or a part of the natural world, but not both. Quite simply, the cube is ours if we altered the space in any way.

Curious minds may be asking why I include the air space here, that immense volume of breathable air above the earth's surface.

Our buildings and other artificial structures enclose a certain volume of the atmosphere above. The blueprints may be two-dimensional, but the building exists in three dimensions.

Or as our faithful Captain Obvious would say: "When you build a building, it isn't fucking flat." A completely flat school would be absurd, after all, clearly preventing the children from reading 'good'.

Buildings also occupy subterranean space below. Early on in our existence our structures sat atop the ground, but you didn't think we could just glue the bottom of that one-kilometer-high skyscraper to the earth's surface, did you?

Some building foundations run decameters deep — more metric fun for you: that's the seldomly used word in between meter and kilometer signifying 10s of meters — and sometimes we put parking garages, storage spaces, machinery, or bad tenants down below the ground line.

We currently take up more physical space than we realize, and cube by cube we are incrementally converting other parts of the natural world into our sphere of influence.

Slowly, gradually, and imperceptibly, we are converting the natural world into our land of make believe. All of these individual pockets that comprise our *humanity bubble* will eventually connect, in theory removing the natural world from the earth altogether.

In theory.

Nature fights us at every turn, though, a never-ending struggle to revert each piece of the *humanity bubble* and the contents within, back to their natural state.

We, of course, fight back, refusing to cede any ground to the wild, and you guessed it, there's an app for that to orchestrate the fight.

Just kidding. We do have a plan, though...

Maintenance

...a maintenance plan!

This *humanity bubble* of ours requires something unique to keep it intact: *maintenance*. Our attempt to keep things in working order.

Makes sense.

Why would we keep a broken vacuum in the closet, or a car on cinder blocks in the driveway? A hole in our roof would provide great natural light into our living space, but a bit of rain changes our opinion really quickly.

We want all of our things to work, and our creations naturally transition to a state of uselessness without periodic human intervention.

Human structures like homes, department stores, or factories become dilapidated once abandoned, slowly absorbed by the natural growth around them. Vines climb walls, roots press through foundations, and animals seek shelter within.

One year my neighbor was actually growing a weed in their basement.

Growing *a* weed, not growing *weed*.

A mint plant pushed its way through the cracks in their foundation, but true to human nature, maintenance to restore the structural integrity of their home outweighed the convenience of harvesting mint indoors.

The pristine, manicured green lawns that come standard around all of our human structures require maintenance too. These patches of manipulated earth do not occur naturally, something I write with confidence as I attempt to block out the sound of the lawnmower army operating throughout my neighborhood, ensuring the aesthetic appeal of dozens of front yards.

In due time, those same landscapers will be back with synthetic fertilizer and grass seed to further maintain the health of that lawn, somehow oblivious to the fact that before the 1940s, open spaces just took care of themselves. No part of that process is natural.

Cars, improperly maintained, simply stop running. See how long you can push off that oil change before you end up with a ruined engine.

Been there. It wasn't fun.

That concrete and asphalt we put everywhere will eventually crumble and give way to the earth below as the natural world tries in vain to unclog its pores of the impurity that is our *humanity bubble*.

My local bike trail became much smoother once our town repaved the path to cover all the protruding roots, but trees are patient and persistent, and their roots once more surfaced a few years later.

Great news for paving companies, though.

Our subterranean pipes slowly decay from outside and within, assaulted from both sides by the treated water running through them and the dirt surrounding them. Sometimes nature even becomes curious, like when tree roots infiltrated the leach field at my childhood home, clogging the small holes in the underground pipes meant to disperse waste from our septic tank.

Apparently, that type of household waste is quite fertile.

There are also a million different types of grease and lubricants that keep things moving throughout our bubble.

I'll close this list by simply stating that any other human construction or fabrication of ours, whether it be mechanical, electrical, pneumatic, hydraulic, structural, or biomedical, will fall into a state of disrepair without proper upkeep.

Nature is patient.

She will wait us out until we tire of this constant fight.

We are perpetually swimming against the riptide, a current we know we should swim *with* to survive, but one we continue to fight against as we insist we know a better way. We can repave, rebuild, repair, and refurbish to our heart's content, but nature continues her effortless rebalancing, and all of our creations will eventually crumble.

Strong and permanent in our naive, young human minds, our clever creations are mere sandcastles built in Father Time's hourglass, sucked down below as time slowly passes.

One way or another, they fall.

With few exceptions — radioactive decay comes to mind, but that's all the research I felt like doing — the natural world for the most part revolves around *growth*, while anything physically made by humans is subject to *decay*.

We stubbornly and relentlessly fight that decay, which leads me to an alternative definition of maintenance:

The human antidote to nature's rejection of all our stuff.

The unnaturalness of this sentence is trumped only by how unnatural the rest of the world views our creations.

We rearrange the elements.

Nature tries to destroy our creations.

We fight back with maintenance.

The concept of *over there*

And now a quick story:

> Two construction managers in adjacent towns continually develop the land within their jurisdictions. Spreading outward, they continue to repurpose undeveloped land for parking lots, buildings, housing, and other human creations.
>
> Each manager beams with pride as they continue to back up, keeping their eyes on their respective masterpieces as they urge the development along to hit their project targets, giving no thought to the origin of their construction materials, and assuming that land to grow food, water sources to quench their thirst, and trees to provide them with air will be maintained elsewhere.
>
> One day both construction workers abruptly bump into something, immediately turning around in disbelief as they realize they bumped into each other.
>
> Too enamored by their own work in front of them, they look past each other and finally lay eyes on the development that had been happening behind them all along. They thought their *essentials* — air, water, and food — could come from *over there* and that they could freely develop their respective immediate surroundings with impunity.
>
> They were wrong.

That passage originated as a prompt to generate an image with AI, but I converted it to a story to skip the excessive energy consumption and challenge you to use your brain to generate the mental image.

Translation: I suck at prompt engineering and I had to pivot.

Over there is that place beyond the horizon we deem impervious to any impacts from our actions right here. The common expression 'out of sight, out of mind' fits, although I'm doing my best to avoid clichés. (Heads up: I will fail miserably.)

I cannot see what's happening? Not my problem, as long as those three essentials just keep showing up from somewhere *over there*.

All those dirty, nasty processes that create the material things we love? Let those happen *over there* too.

We put up a wall at the *point of receipt*, that arbitrary and invisible dividing line between where our personal effort to obtain something ends, and the external effort required to deliver us that product or service begins.

We optimize our *humanity bubble* to minimize the former, regardless of the immense supply chain footprint growing behind the curtain to maximize personal convenience.

It's fine.

It's all *over there*, and last I checked, the earth is really fucking big, so there's plenty of space.

We selfishly assume elsewhere takes care of us, refusing to realize the people who exist *over there* are thinking the same thing we are, and once we metaphorically bump into each other like those two construction workers, there's only one place left to go.

The great outdoors

Driving through the mountains of northern Vermont one summer, I admired the verdant landscape and struggled to maintain my lane as I appreciated the beautiful vistas of myriad trees on sparsely developed land in this area. Thankfully all that mountainous terrain prevents the dense development normally seen in flatter parts of the world.

Unspoiled nature. Such an incredible sight for a recluse like me.

Then my inner Debbie Downer kicked in, and it dawned on me that this area hasn't been developed *today*, simply because a cost-effective way to develop such terrain simply doesn't exist yet. Give it 50 years, I tell myself, once the rest of the easily developed parcels run out, and someone will get creative.

It's just what we do.

Until then though, this land remains untouched. A part of the good ol' outdoors: any undeveloped place outside of our *humanity bubble* we purportedly protect. Somehow most governments, a few NGOs, and a handful of altruistic people have forever preserved national parks and other areas.

Allegedly.

I am forever skeptical of that *forever* word.

In our minds the remaining untouched land is out there in reserve until needed for human development or resources.

In the meantime, we happily head *out* to the great outdoors.

We escape reality and head *out* into the mountains.

We collectively view the natural world, the wilderness, as a completely different place, a distinct destination that we prefer to watch on screens as we insist that experiencing nature is best enjoyed with only two out of our five senses.

We also tell ourselves we can't get hurt from the couch, instead subjecting our bodies to the gradual damage caused by spending a good portion of our lives in a seated position. We are scared off by the highly consequential but very unlikely risk of being mauled by a bear as we happily accept a partially fused spine decades from now caused by all that sitting.

Even if we wander out, we always come back because humans are tethered to this *humanity bubble*.

If you brave the wilderness and prove your ability to last out there, then you are a *survivalist*. Or, taken from the perspective of every other species on this planet, you escaped and returned to reality.

The space between

We envision an impenetrable boundary between our little *humanity bubble* and the outdoors.

"Get on outta here!" with all that outdoors-y stuff. Nothing comes in or out unless we say so.

Our artificial and ordered *humanity bubble* exists on one side, while the chaotic and wild natural world exists on the other. Natural ecosystems seamlessly integrate with each other, but we sever all connection points and take control to spread our greatness.

Recalling that painful 3-D cube analogy from earlier, there isn't one single boundary or crossover point between our *humanity bubble* and the natural world. There are endless dividing lines everywhere.

Some boundaries are abstract; others are more concrete.

Some boundaries are literally concrete. It's everywhere, appearing alongside our other favorite construction material: asphalt.

We isolate ourselves from all other forms of life on the planet that we haven't domesticated. We seal up our houses and buildings to prevent anything from invading our domain, while lawns surrounding our houses and buildings create an additional buffer between our world and the natural world.

When we grow plants in pots, we've created a boundary between plant roots and the earth to which they have always connected. Same with a rooftop garden. An admirable pursuit, but one that still puts a very large human structure between the plant and the earth's surface.

Our gardens on the ground may be connected to the earth below, but we also put up fences to prevent animal intruders.

Shoes on our feet sever the connection between body and earth, with progressively thicker soles increasing the separation.

Our clothing creates another barrier between our skin and the air.

Our automobiles, little bubbles on wheels, allow us to bring our perfect conditions — our safe space — with us wherever we go. Then we have our RVs, some of which rival the size of a typical home of centuries past, allowing us to pretend we're outdoors for multiple days at a time despite still enjoying our comforts.

We put up our borders around our *humanity bubble* to guard our way of life as best we can, but sometimes we cannot hold the line.

When the boundary is breached

What happens when the outdoors comes a-knockin'? What happens when nature in particular violates our *humanity bubble* boundaries?

Fires.

Hurricanes.

Tornadoes.

Thunderstorms.

Blizzards.

Avalanches.

Earthquakes.

Landslides.

Floods.

Sinkholes.

Despite our best efforts, nature inevitably crashes through our seemingly impermeable walls. These sad occurrences continue to surprise us, at times leaving us feeling insulted that the planet would have the audacity to mess with our stuff. As if these events are completely unexpected and specifically targeted at us, and haven't been constant throughout the history of earth.

We see it as an attack on our way of life, an inexplicable invasion of our *humanity bubble* that we falsely deem impervious to catastrophe as we forget that these events are standard for nature.

Hurricane Katrina was terrible, but it was just another Monday. Actually, it was just another day, since there is no evidence that Mother Nature ever adopted our calendar system.

Everything in our bubble requires an explanation, though – the guilty party toward which we point our fingers and our lawsuits. Someone or something to blame and eventually sue over the outcome. That's why, despite natural disasters being—well—natural, and having no real source, we call them 'acts of God' in our insurance paperwork, satisfying our need to identify a responsible party.

We cannot possibly fathom that shit can just *happen* out there in the natural world, leading us to label these occurrences as *disasters*. Natural *disasters*. Nature is powerful, it is unpredictable, and it does not give a damn about our precious things.

The energy the natural world effortlessly harnesses can be difficult to articulate, so if you ever find yourself in the vicinity of Niagara Falls, please go stand at approximately 43° - 04' - 44.1" north by 79° - 04' - 41.3" west, on the Canadian side, and you can feel the raw power of nature as the water rushes over the precipice.

Our Push Out of Balance with Nature

First of one

"Look at that cat over there, just lying around doing nothing all day. Get a job!"

Two thoughts immediately crossed my mind as I casually mumbled those words one day:

1. I am criticizing a cat. I should probably move up that therapy appointment.

2. What if that cat is doing life right?

That internal exchange formed the basis for this book, as I considered the possibility that *humans* are actually the ones behaving oddly.

Maybe we are the outlier.

We strive to remain atop the species hierarchy, hastily reshaping the planet to benefit our species at the expense of others. We sprint onward, overly paranoid that inferior creatures are after our throne, and in the process consume what the earth has graciously bestowed on the planet for all in an effort to guard our apex status. Maybe it's time for a standings update to see who is currently winning this race.

Great news, we are easily in first place. Cue the chants everybody:

"hu-MAN-i-TY ... hu-MAN-i-TY!"

Don't pop the champagne yet, though — we are simply first in a race of one. Other species aren't competing.

We are alone on the starting block, with no one else attempting to advance like us, presumably choosing instead to maintain their natural equilibrium and remain in harmony with nature.

That cat I ridiculed wasn't contemplating its inferiority as I told it to be more productive. It was more likely wondering why the hell a lifeform so clearly dependent on external sustenance is so reckless with its energy expenditure.

Meanwhile, we're riding high, intoxicated by our success and basking in our amazingness while seemingly unaware of any potential catastrophe. That looming possibility of our world falling out from under our feet, and given how many sinkholes keep appearing in my general area, there seems to be a legitimate likelihood of the earth literally falling out from under us at any moment.

We are perpetually growing an unnatural subsystem on this planet, our personal species safe house from which we reach out into the natural world and take without giving back. Blazing our own trail, operating under the impression that we know better than every other species on this planet — and eons of history — refusing to look back and see that we are not even in a race at all.

For a species so obsessed with golf, you'd think we'd easily recognize a scoring system where less is better.

I question how our way is better as I sit in an unnatural position for half my waking hours on a human object (chair) while using another human creation (computer) positioned awkwardly on yet another human invention (desk) to create unimportant work products (those deliverable things) in exchange for an imaginary reward (that currency stuff) that *then* allows me to buy the very real essentials that for eons my ancestors could just obtain if they sought them out.

Brilliant revelation, or further signs of my mid-life 'not-a-crisis' materializing? We'll see.

We think we are uniquely capable of doing what we do, but the entire natural world probably considered it, then questioned who in their right mind would make their lives so insanely fucking complicated.

We really didn't think this one through, this relentless push of ours out of balance with the rest of the system.

Fire!

The full phrase is "Ready, Aim, Fire!" but in our creative process we are never truly *ready*, and we sure as hell don't even bother *aiming* anymore. Just *fire* away as quickly as we can to be first. We recklessly push the limits in the name of progress and innovation, using a simple two-question barometer for pursuing a new endeavor:

1. Can I sell it for more than it will cost to produce it?

2. Will it break any existing laws?

Clear those two hurdles, and it's off to the races.

I intentionally left out the question, "Is it needed?" because societally we have no concept of what truly constitutes a need anymore. Another additional question for some of our more conceited species members would be to ask if our planned creations would break any records, resulting in our billion-dollar skyscrapers swaying in the breeze, and the groundbreaking convex glass façade on that other building redirecting sunlight downward and literally breaking the ground as it melts the sidewalk.

We make no proactive attempt to evaluate the long-term implications of our new innovations, reevaluating our decisions in hindsight and *then* making adjustments, as evidenced by a few common examples from recent history that we know and love:

- Doctors smoked in patient rooms.

- Asbestos was a great building material.

- Lead (the metal) seemed like a great fuel additive and a cheap building material for our water pipes.

- Those forever chemicals simplified our lives and saved our elbows by reducing the need to scrub our frying pans clean.

- Single-use water bottles, bags, and other plastics were a great way to get something on the run quickly and conveniently.

We interpret passing of today's standards as approval in perpetuity, and finding a product on the shelf implies approval to use liberally without consequence. If that wasn't the case, someone would certainly prevent us from such blatant misuse.

We get the all-clear in the moment from some regulatory body, legally document the clearance as proof we are allowed to do it right now, and then skip the part where we consider the long-term consequences. Research by the original creator stops and their attention shifts toward their next new product.

Put it out there now and someone else can address the consequences.

Don't put it out there and we are left behind, stagnating if we don't pursue perpetual ingenuity.

But would stagnation be such a bad thing?

Feedback lag

We are programmed to seek feedback.

Feedback from our boss.

From our colleagues.

From our customers ("Tell us how we did!" "Leave a review!" "Like and subscribe!").

From our romantic partners.

From our friends.

These situations are pretty clear. In the work scenario, we establish goals, perform tasks, witness results within a year, discuss our performance (sometimes), and make changes for next year.

Rinse and repeat.

For.

Your.

Entire.

Career.

The feedback from our partners may seem convoluted — I'm no easy one myself — but we'll call that one relatively straightforward.

Our social environment trains us to expect direct and fairly immediate feedback, but there are situations where consequences are less obvious. As we slide down the 'straightforwardness scale' a bit, we see how feedback can vary in complexity:

- Accidentally cut yourself with a kitchen knife while chopping scallions, and you *immediately* know you messed up. That shit hurts. The blood that was previously in your body where it belongs is now on the cutting board, and it appears part of your fingerprint is dangling off your pinky finger. It is quite clearly time to seek medical attention, and those scallions certainly cannot be used in your meal.

- Sometimes you don't realize until the *next morning* that you had one too many cocktails the night before. Whether you make better decisions next time is another matter, but the various body aches you experience hours later clearly tie to what you consumed last night.

- When your drinking water tastes salty in the winter, you realize *a few weeks later* that the salt-filled runoff from your town roadways has somehow made its way into the water supply.

- Eat like crap one day, and you probably won't notice anything right away. If you're a teen, it won't even phase you. Keep eating that way for *a few months*, especially if you're nearing your 40s, and you suddenly look down and can't see your feet. A small group of humans with a certain external reproductive appendage below the belt may use a different visual cue, but the feedback timeline remains unchanged.

- Go the other way and start up at the gym and you'll likewise see nothing changing at the onset, until changes finally start to happen *three to four months* later.

Now that we've discussed my gym habits, my inability to chop vegetables without cutting myself, someone else's drinking problem, and my town's drinking [water] problem, let's really push the limits with a crazy hypothetical work scenario.

What if we were performing a task without knowing the boss, without understanding the goals or impacts of our immediate actions to help guide us, without being told our actions will be compounded with the actions of other people we do not know...

...and we won't receive feedback until half a century from now?

Who in their right mind would care?

Half a century is a full career in the human world, and an eternity when compared to the quarter-year segments that track our lives. Feedback at this frequency arrives after we retire or even after we're dead, so that sounds like a problem for the next person.

While this hypothetical professional scenario is—well—hypothetical, we can use it to better approximate how nature operates.

There can be a significant delay between our actions and the corresponding consequences. Seemingly inconsequential decisions today can affect something miles away decades from now due to countless variables driving completely unpredictable outcomes.

Have you heard that one about a butterfly flapping its wings on one continent and causing a hurricane on another? It is a preposterous, highly exaggerated, and oddly plausible statement once you delve into all the systemic life connections.

We incorrectly believe that since a human life unnaturally lasts about a century, the rest of the planet must operate on that same timescale.

Personally, I'll be long dead by the year 2140, so I won't see the long-term consequences of my actions. I can deal with the direct, near-term stuff, but if nothing immediately happens, then so what?

If I chop down a tree and nothing immediately happens, I proceed until my entire building site is devoid of life, giving no thought to the impact of killing in a day plants that took decades to grow.

Something changed.

Trees were there, and now they are not, but we take the absence of immediate, direct consequence as an indication that there will be *no* consequence whatsoever, ever.

Considering those trees are quite well known for producing one of the essentials of life on this planet, any astute observer should conclude that cutting down too many of them will not be great.

We laugh at the imbecile frog that doesn't jump out of the pot of water as the temperature slowly and imperceivably rises to a boil, yet we foolishly behave in a similar manner on a planetary scale.

At least the frog merely takes its own life out of ignorance as it fails to recognize what we would consider glaringly obvious feedback that something is amiss. Meanwhile our dumbass species keeps knowingly destroying the primary living organism that allows us to breathe.

We act as if we exist in a video game that lacks the appropriate physics engine to properly emulate the real world, allowing us to assume no consequence to our actions in this living system.

We beat the systems thing to death already, but systems require balance and they rely on feedback to maintain that balance. Consequences ensue without equilibrium, such as when a single species imposes their better way on their surrounding environment.

We just cannot help it — we never know when to quit.

Unlocking enough

It's never enough.

I know, I know.

Don't use *it* without context in a standalone sentence. I should also avoid contractions too, so apologies once more to my English teachers because I do this throughout the book. In this case, though, the ambiguity is kind of the point.

It in this context is pretty much anything.

We fail to truly understand what it means to have enough, and our inability to feel any sense of contentment whatsoever drives our relentless and disharmonizing advancement.

As the constantly moving satisfaction finish line continues to outpace us, we trudge along on our endless quest to cross it, unaware of the dwindling resource stockpile we exhaust in the process.

We also transitioned to seeking possessions in the virtual world under the assumption that the bits and bytes underpinning that environment are harmless. Once more we find ourselves oblivious to the real-world impacts, seemingly incapable of comprehending the fact that virtual consumption adversely affects the physical planet.

Maybe it's ignorance. Maybe it's avarice.

Perhaps we are just asking the wrong question.

We ask ourselves: "How much *is enough?*"

We should be asking ourselves: "What will enough *feel like* once I've achieved it?"

We hopelessly seek a numerical answer to a qualitative, emotional question. *Enough* is a feeling, yet we insist we achieve it by first predicting how much of an arbitrary resource we'll need decades from now, and then we relentlessly pursue that target until we die.

Enough is an innate sense that we've bastardized in our pursuit of material and immaterial possessions. You feel it, you don't quantify it.

It is also a shifting state. You can come in and out of having enough, guided by how you *feel* at any given moment. I didn't quit my job to critique our species because the math worked. I just felt satisfied with my life at that decision point.

I had a feeling, and I ran with it.

I also may have heard the words "It's a valid order, so we're following it" from a superior when I challenged an inane work requirement, but that definitely didn't influence my decision to leave at all.

I left because of a feeling, nothing more.

I intrinsically felt comfortable and secure, and quite honestly I wanted a break from working for someone else.

That feeling can change, though, and adjustments are necessary. Despite my desire to stay retired forever at this ripe old age of 29 and holding, I will eventually go back.

Another bold strategy here — I'm not calling this abrupt upending of my professional life a crisis in any way.

Our species speedometer is pegged at a million kilometers an hour, and we refuse to decelerate despite the dearth of pursuers on the racetrack. We ignore the pit stops as they fly by, which would be fine if our wheels weren't currently on fire.

Our next closest competitor in our personal world-building game is probably a beaver and their damn dams. Perhaps not. More complex examples may exist, but using beavers set the stage nicely for a mediocre 'dam' joke here.

Thanks to Cousin Eddie for the inspiration.

Having failed to come up with a witty transition to follow that cult movie reference, I will simply say it is time to start exploring specific human behaviors. I leave you with one last question to consider as you flip the page:

What would enough *feel* like to you?

Our Relationship with the Planet

We consciously reorganize the elements

Look around for a moment and find something made by humans.

This task is not hard. If nothing else you have this book, but if you some-how *don't* see anything human-made, please tell me the location so I can consider moving there.

No need to drop an exact pin — I'll spare you the creepy old man vibes and immediately concede that I'd run back home after a day without electricity.

While other species 'make' things by digging a few subterranean tunnels or weaving a few sticks together to block a river, no one else is rearranging the elements on a molecular level quite like us.

When did we start this practice? I say our species' first exploration tinkering with the elements was with making fire.

Some would argue that Prometheus handed us fire on a silver platter.

Others credit Maui.

Pragmatic types might believe that a pair of romantically involved cave-people started fighting, stones started flying across the cave, and sparks literally flew when an errant rock hit the cave wall.

Whatever narrative works for you.

At any rate, fire is great. Rub a few sticks together over some dry leaves, the spark ignites, and hopefully you've taken precautions to prevent the surrounding forest from descending into an inferno.

We progressively used this wonderful chemical reaction to keep warm, see at night, ward off predators, cook our food, burn at the stake those whose advanced intelligence frightened us, and who knows what else.

From there we continued to surf the wave of human innovation, giving rise to a host of other revolutionary discoveries. Skipping over the minutiae in the same way I glazed over my high school history textbooks, we will simply run through a condensed list of major milestones that have drastically altered human life: agriculture, metallurgy, steel, electricity, and our modern inventions like computing and AI.

We cannot forget gunpowder either. We somehow learned through what I can only assume was trial and error that if you contain or pressurize that mystical fire-stuff that we harnessed, you can create a lot of crazy things that can fly a long way and/or go boom.

Fireworks come to mind as the first success story in this department, but then we got a little more creative.

Humans are master manipulators of the elements, those 118 little squares representing every chemical element known to our species, meticulously arranged in true Type-A fashion throughout the periodic table that you probably forgot from school.

For those that were initially thinking I was talking about the weather by referencing how we manipulate the *elements*, fear not, as we are in fact on the brink of manipulating the clouds to cause a desert deluge.

Limited by nothing more than these elements and our imaginations, we continually follow the standard *script of advancement* that first acknowledges the greatness of our creations, and then immediately asks what comes next. Don't ask me specifically what's next though, because if I knew I would be writing a patent application instead of this silly book. What I can say definitively is that *something* new and innovative is coming.

We simply cannot help ourselves.

Our ingenuity knows no bounds. We have created without question the most impressive new technologies that have graced this planet, or depending on your vantage point, degraded it.

We are actually the only species to create *any* technology whatsoever.

Technology, a human concept, exists to sustain our *humanity bubble*, and we have trained an army of problem solvers to lead the charge.

I was one of them.

Our Engineering 'High'

Engineering school was brutal.

Seriously. It really sucked.

Endless calculations, labs, experiments, eight days a week worth of homework, definitely no parties, and a grading curve that defied all logic. My 38/100 on that Aerospace Propulsion final was actually a B?

How did I end up on such a path, one might ask? Well, it went something like this:

"Hey Brian, you're pretty good at math and you like building things with blocks. You should be an engineer!"

Being a man of many words and deep convictions, someone who at that time knew himself well and walked his own path free of any outside influence, decisively replied:

"Okay."

It seemed like a prestigious path at the time, and since I was a self-proclaimed problem solver who was happy to have someone else point the way, it was a perfect match.

The honeymoon is over, though, and that engineering label is no longer applicable as I recently reevaluated that term with a new lens.

Engineering from the standard vantage point is more or less using technical knowledge and experience to find suitable solutions to a particular problem. In a nutshell, engineers take all that theoretical science and physics stuff and make something useful with it.

That's great, but what is a *problem*? What is *useful*?

A true *problem* in our not-so-distant past — and likely once again in the near future with the way things are going today — would be something like: "Where am I going to find food today?"

This thought is not as absurd as you may think. Remember the COVID years.

We've significantly stretched our definition of the word *problem*, indistinctly drifting from finding our basic needs toward shaving milliseconds off our computer processing times, and I've consequently formed a new hypothesis on engineering:

Today's engineering solutions merely address the side effects of implementing yesterday's engineering solutions, with this cause-effect relationship dating back to our harnessing fire.

Now remember, this is a hypothesis. *An* hypothesis?

Stupid h-words next to an indefinite article. One of those is right.

Grammar aside, my statement is simply a proposed explanation or educated guess that can and should be tested, a tentative suggestion that we are stuck in a perpetual engineering 'do-loop' of sorts. A state of constant iteration with no exit conditions to stop our growth.

All of our fancy stuff inevitably causes side effects, and we create new things to address those unintended outcomes instead of just stopping our actions at the source.

Our collective sense of superiority convinces us that we have an entitlement to all previous discoveries in perpetuity. Each new advancement is a basic video game checkpoint, where progress is saved and there is no need to regress once we achieve our current place. We actually convince ourselves regression isn't even an option.

With presumably no other choice, we march on in the name of progress and stubbornly hold our ground with our creations. If we find that detrimental effects arise later from some new implementation, our default mindset is to keep the thing we just made and simply engineer a solution to the new problem it created.

It's almost like our constant focus on engineering problems allows us to avoid a sophisticated set of psychological or behavioral problems that we can't see, or more likely just ignore, in the background.

Regardless of the validity of that armchair quarterback psychological evaluation — I'm definitely not a psychologist — the cycle continues, which would be perfectly fine if our main focus was building utopia.

But it's not. Just look at where we focus our engineering efforts.

En Garde… ou attaque?

The Christmas Truce of 1914 was an informal agreement near the beginning of World War I where French, British, and German soldiers laid down their arms for two days to celebrate Christmas.

They resumed fighting on the third day.

Why the hell did they resume fighting!?!

From sharing bullets to beers to bombs over the course of 72 hours? That's absolutely bonkers, yet somehow also completely sensible, because human nature all but guarantees that the one who lays down their weapon and walks away definitely gets shot in the back.

Paranoia for the win.

No other species has come close to harnessing the power of fire, let alone dropping an atom bomb, which is fine since one species dropping bombs is more than enough.

Admittedly, we legitimately needed weapons at some point to hunt and defend ourselves.

If you follow human evolution, each age had its standard implements of destruction. Hitting a few of the highlights, we start with clubs and spears, move on to crossbows and broadswords, and then venture into the gunpowder age before eventually arriving at our modern weapon of choice: guns, with an honorable mention for bombs at the nation-state level.

If you *don't* follow human evolution, then we received all these weapons through next-day delivery. They were suddenly just there.

Getting back to that transition to gunpowder, that was also about the time we started exponentially increasing our kill rate.

We started by creatively impaling a single living creature to feed or defend ourselves, and a few short millennia later our weapons contain sufficient power to wipe portions of the earth's surface bare.

Such power, and we love wielding it. We must, right? Why else would we spend so much of our supposedly limited resources on obtaining it?

Why else would we reveal new weapon systems with the same fervor as introducing the headlining musical act at a concert?

Upbeat, energetic intro music, intricate light shows, fog machines, a suspenseful crescendo combined with the unexpected dropping of a large banner suspended from the rafters to reveal what hides on stage.

Is it [insert your favorite artist] standing up there behind that curtain, ready to belt out their new hit single?

Nope — it's a fucking tank.

Even the most devout pacifist must concede that weapons have always existed, from those first clubs and spears of bygone eras to our combined global nuclear arsenals today — a little over a myriad of them, by last approximation — but we now celebrate the ability to inflict mass carnage while pretty much every other species on the planet uses what they have on their bodies for hunting and defense.

How would we fare if we had to fend for ourselves with nothing but our bare hands?

I'd be screwed.

Even the deer we constantly hunt with our bows, firearms, and vehicles would impale us with their antlers if given the opportunity. I was stuck on a small mountain in Canada for 30 minutes once because I didn't want to startle the buck that followed me up the hill and blocked my only exit route. It was amazing how I automatically switched from admiring the peaceful landscape to wishing for a rifle or at least a knife the moment I locked eyes with that beast.

Beast.

It is quite weird thinking of a deer as a beast. We either see them from afar and they appear small, or on TV and they appear kind, or on the road and they appear—well—dead. We may also see them on someone's wall, where they appear completely harmless, but also dead. Despite our standard accepted perceptions of deer from the safety of our bubble, they are impressive creatures when we find ourselves defenseless in their presence out in nature.

Without weapons we are weak.

Without weapons we are helpless.

Maybe our fingernails at one time served a better purpose for hunting? Certainly not now, though. Our brittle, fragile little calcium-daggers buckle when trying to open a soda can.

They look nice though, especially when we paint them.

Our teeth may have been sharper at one point and could penetrate the flesh of the things we ate, but not now. We have a steak knife for that, and we also put that fire stuff to good use to soften up our food before we eat it.

They look nice, though, especially when we straighten and whiten them.

Lions and Tigers and Bears have claws and teeth — Last 'wizard...' reference, I promise.

Wasps have a stinger.

Deer have antlers.

Birds have a beak, and maybe talons.

Narwhals have a wicked sharp horn-looking thing that I always forget is actually a tooth protruding out through their upper lip.

Humans have MOABs though, so that's good. An official, jargony definition exists, but the playful designers ensured the acronym also fit their colloquial interpretation: 'Mother of All Bombs.'

We focus on survival against all the other human clans in this little 'real-life' video game within our *humanity bubble*, while ignoring our collective long-term survival as a species in the natural world.

We seem to have our priorities in order.

We know damn well that we are weak, feeble, and naturally unarmed, so we had to engineer ways to kill off any other species that threatened us.

Our greatest insecurity is our inability to defend ourselves. Maybe that's why we go overboard in our *humanity bubble* with all those weapons, and then call it defense?

Weapons production is lucrative, and organizations advertise their lethality 24/7/365 the same way other companies mundanely advertise their valves and pumps and pipes.

It's all just a big game.

Until someone gets hurt.

Which someone always does, because they are weapons, and it's war. It's war veiled as defense. Observe our subtle naming conventions.

Defense industry.

Defense spending.

Defense Secretary.

Defense Department.

Defense Ministry.

Defense strategy.

Defense Minister.

How the hell are we all somehow on defense?

If you had two teams on a football pitch — the real football by the way, the one where you are predominantly kicking a *ball* with your *foot* — and both teams remained on defense, the ball would remain in the center and every player would just idly hang on their respective sides blocking their nets.

Someone is lying. *Someone* has to be on offense.

Conveniently enough, one major nation was unofficially rebranding from *Defense* to *War* just as I was drafting this book. Lovely timing, and a puzzling choice for a group of supposed promoters of peace.

Welcome to the perpetual 'superpower-noia' cycle.

The superior group reigning over the world inevitably becomes so paranoid and insecure in the thought that others are out to dethrone them that they perpetually build up their arsenal. As a surprise to nobody except apparently the superior group, other groups follow suit because duh, if the top dog is preparing for battle, those lagging behind better do the same because being 2nd or worse logically indicates they are already outmatched.

Tensions eventually escalate until war ensues and the cycle repeats.

And it will continue to repeat, because those that refuse to face the war inside will forever project that fight outward. Unwilling to challenge the demons within, we forego the hard work of finding inner peace in exchange for the significantly easier task of identifying and ostracizing an external scapegoat.

A person.

A people.

A nation.

Anything but ourselves. We couldn't possibly be the problem.

I am all for process improvement, but far too much energy and resources are spent figuring out better ways to kill each other. Imagine a world where we devote some of those resources to something more mutually beneficial. A world where humans integrate with nature and support growth instead of death and decay.

Sensing an impending loss of my readers with all this 'rainbows and butterflies' rhetoric, I'll cease further talk of that silly pipe dream.

Just give it some thought.

Speaking of all those resources, though, where are we finding all of this raw material to make these things of ours?

Oh, right...

We lay claim to the land

It's tough to move around with baggage, and bullets are really heavy, so we gave up our nomadic lifestyle and chose to settle down.

Anchored by our things, and clamoring for ownership of this other thing that "they're just not making any more of" these days, we planted ourselves in one place.

We own the land now.

Representatives from other species did not attend deliberations on the land ownership matter, so we assumed sole land rights through a default judgement.

Just kidding.

How ridiculous, the thought of an inter-species tribunal negotiating land rights. We made that decision unilaterally, and surveyors immediately started drawing property lines.

We placed first in the evolutionary race to the top, beating out all zero competitors in this race of one, and as our prize we granted ourselves ownership of the land. Here we are a short while later, wrapping up the first quarter of the 21st century and easily able to account for nearly every square meter on this rock.

With the land ownership matter settled — deeds issued, maps drawn — we put up our fences, staked our flags in the ground, built our walls, and began leaving our mark on the physical world. The entire surface of the earth is now meticulously organized into mostly undisputed parcels very clearly indicating to humans who owns what.

Our maps keep track of it all, but our cartographical theatrics ignore one critical issue.

We don't actually own the land.

We think we do.

We made legal documents that say we do, and therefore declare our claims irrefutable.

But we truly own nothing.

Ownership is a human construct. Those legal documents, also a strictly human creation, only hold value in our *humanity bubble*. Nearly every other species on this planet would sooner eat the paper on which those words are printed than obey what it says, because they are meaningless to every other living creature and the rest of the natural world.

Nevertheless, with our legal permission slips in hand, we carved up this planet to our liking, bringing to life our little dream land.

For sale. For lease. Build to suit

With ownership comes the ability to sell, and just like that, all that land we took for ourselves now has a monetary value. We even established a standard means for quantifying land value to help with those transactions. How does that standard work, you ask?

Who the hell knows.

I just looked at my estimated home value and cannot comprehend the number they claim. It's arbitrary, undoubtedly inflated, and just like every other property value on the planet, it is missing one key ingredient.

Incapable of expressing our essentials in math terms, we fail to factor into that standard any contributions that the land was making to keep living species alive, which seems like an acceptable omission that we can live with until we remember that *we* are one of those species that the land so generously keeps alive.

Our input variables for that value calculation only factor in the potential monetary impact of that land within our *humanity bubble.*

But how do we quantify our essentials to round out the calculation?

You don't.

You can't, actually, and that's kind of the whole point here.

It is a fundamental and possibly intentional incompatibility. One would think we could collectively conclude that destroying the thing keeping us alive is a bad call, but other motivators drive our decisions.

We simply quantify the opportunity cost of *not* using the land — "I could make $x / month with that land, so by leaving it undeveloped I am losing that same amount" — which leads us to the impossible comparison of a known, quantitative, near-term, direct monetary loss in our *humanity bubble* against an unknown qualitative, long-term, mostly indirect environmental gain out in reality.

No one has managed to create a direct translation, making any claim to environmental benefits indefensible simply because we can't express it with a number.

Part of the quantification issue may be that we can't identify the tree that produced the specific molecules we inhale at any given moment. I confidently state this claim because if we *could* identify the source of our air, I would already have, alongside my water bill and food bill, an 'air bill' from that tree owner invoicing me for the air that I breathe.

Land is a commodity now. A mere product changing hands like trading cards, and we consistently build to suit, because land makes more money when developed.

Something needs to be there.

A housing unit.

A strip mall.

A dollar store.

An amusement park.

A skyscraper.

A coffee shop.

A parking lot.

While a mound of dirt is great for sledding in the winter if it snows where you live, it doesn't pay the bills.

Apparently using the land to grow food isn't enough to pay the bills either. Offer a shit-ton of money to a farmer in exchange for the land they backbreakingly work to grow food for a meager salary, and what do you think will happen?

Poof. The local farm is suddenly a townhome community. Both corn fields near my childhood home are now housing developments, and while corn may not be the best crop, at least the land was growing something edible back then.

Demanding that all land generates money drives us to transfer additional land from the natural world into our *humanity bubble*. Land that would otherwise support earth's basic functions suddenly becomes a parking garage.

We aren't making more land — remember? — so this situation is very much zero sum. Simple addition and subtraction. Adding 10 hectares into our *humanity bubble* removes 10 hectares from the natural world.

More brashly, we're breaking the very systems that keep us alive to generate income that contributes to our high score in this "Will I have enough money to last until I die?" game of ours.

Humans occasionally consider environmental factors during development due to legislation and regulation, but most enforcement attempts are met with something like what I've experienced over the past few decades, which is incessant bitching and moaning — venting, as it's more eloquently known in professional circles — about the project hold-up resulting from an environmental study.

Even the multi-million-dollar addition to my high school was delayed due to a snake or bird living in the proposed construction zone. At that time, we high schoolers didn't care, we just wanted an updated school. Annoyed back then that the animal delayed project completion until one year after I graduated, with hindsight I would have preferred to leave the animal alone.

Environmental studies and evaluations draw disdain because they slow our ability to develop the land, generate revenue, and provide us with value in our *humanity bubble*.

Organizations, those business entities that are somehow also considered people, count the dollars they are losing each day with construction delays as creditors circle to collect their debt payments, and governments follow to collect their taxes.

Land works for us now, and we won't tolerate it being idle, even though that land being idle is the exact state that keeps countless natural systems running.

Are environmental studies effective?

Maybe.

Regardless, they are just a band-aid that distracts us from responsibly addressing our distorted view of land's true purpose.

And beyond our bubble we have Mother Nature with the most puzzled of looks on her face, wondering what the hell her prized creation is doing destroying the vital components to all life on the planet just to have another mall.

Controlling all that remains

Despite Mother Nature's exasperated foot-stomping and face-palming, construction is complete and we must now decide the fate of the dirty mess surrounding our new creation.

We don't feel like walking through the bare dirt. We don't even want to look at it, so definitely put down some sod on that naked land. Plants would be great too, but which ones? We could just wait to see what grows, but that takes too long, and who knows if it'll even look nice when it finally grows in.

Instead, we dictate what grows in those seemingly natural parts of our *humanity bubble* that we think represent nature.

In the true natural world, *whatever grows goes*, since that whole Darwin-based survival thing applies to plant species too.

The ground will naturally promote the growth of native flora barring no human intervention. Humans can't help but butt in, though, and we start moving plants around to our liking, which leads to palm trees in PA, cacti in Maine, evergreens in the Caribbean, and meticulously manicured rose gardens just about everywhere.

Care to have a little fun?

Dig up a one-square-meter patch of your yard, leave it as bare dirt for six months, and observe what happens.

If you are inexplicably overprotective of that award-winning lawn out there, and are appalled at the thought of disturbing even a small portion of it for this test, just drive by a cleared building site that is awaiting construction while whatever bureaucratic nonsense we've restrained ourselves with is reconciled.

You'll see the same outcome.

Something will grow.

Life, in some form, just finds a way.

That sage advice brought to you by a nineties blockbuster movie that pretty blatantly epitomizes why we shouldn't screw around with the natural order too much.

#dinosaurs and what not.

Humans are picky. We don't like all forms of life, so we identified what plant species can exist in our *humanity bubble* and now place them in a very specific, orderly way that is pleasing to the Type-A eye.

We spray any plants we deem unworthy with weed killer, and then pat ourselves on the back for eliminating a supposed threat.

Decades later it finally occurs to us that a spray that instantaneously and indiscriminately eviscerates *every living thing* in its path might actually attack human cells as well, leading us to finally question any use of the word 'safe' in that product's marketing.

Who knew? At least the weeds are gone, though.

If you have such a visceral reaction toward the presence of a weed, maybe go smoke some weed instead and chill out, if you are in a position to legally partake in the budding practice.

We grow up more or less knowing how our areas should look. Landscaping beds with specific plants near the house selected from what's available at a local store. A lush green lawn out front and back, maybe a tree or two, but we don't want too much shade. Keep the grass at a specific height, arrange our landscaping in neatly ordered rows of plants, trim our bushes to exact proportions, and sometimes even mold them into weird shapes.

An adjacent neighborhood has a bush — or maybe it's a shrubbery? — in the shape of a dinosaur next to their driveway.

Last dinosaur reference, I promise.

In the little space that remains open, we prioritize growth of plant species that serve aesthetic purposes over growing edible plants.

Why do we choose plants that satisfy our eyes and not our stomachs?

Easy.

The misleading notion that an ample amount of our necessities will consistently come from *over there*, and the constant reassurances we receive that everything we need to eat and drink will always be within a few miles of us. As long as we earn enough money to buy it by altering our world right here — and another pandemic stays away — our essentials will always be available.

What's eaten is grown somewhere else, packaged up, and shipped to the local grocery store where it is available for purchase.

What's grown in our yards is dictated by societal pressure to be aesthetically pleasing.

What's grown on our farms is controlled through subsidies set by the same governmental body that changes its mind every couple of years or so about which bathroom it thinks we should use.

Witnessing that level of shenanigans is worth at least one tomato plant in your backyard, just in case.

That lush green grass though

How does the end of a world war give rise to the weird green lawns we know today?

"Well, the war's over, wtf do we do with all of these chemical factories?"

Unsubstantiated claim: we have the lawns we have today because nobody wanted to decommission all those ammonium nitrate plants from World War II. We must use them for something to avoid that technological regression we talked about.

Checkpoint cleared, no turning back now!

The chemicals for bombs closely resemble what plants require to grow — I guess? — so maybe we can invent something that is inexplicably utilized multiple times a year forever, consequently generating recurring income for the factory owner.

Boom.

Fertilizer is unleashed to the masses, but instead of it going boom, it gave rise to the monoculture lawns of today, as we began marketing to the individual homeowner a new and revolutionary type of plant food that quickly and abundantly grows an inedible plant species.

This new discovery also still goes boom sometimes, though, so don't store too much in one place.

Nobody needed that type of lawn, but here we are with a front yard fashion statement that wasn't necessarily demanded or requested by anyone. It does nothing more than keep our easily offended eyes and dainty bare feet comfortable, and makes our sports easier since it is quite difficult to putt when the grass is too long.

A lucrative idea for the *humanity bubble*, but a detriment to the natural world and a choice we collectively make every day. I made it for years, realizing in hindsight that one of the first things I did when I purchased my home was to purchase grass seed and fertilizer at the hardware store. I didn't even realize I was doing it, and I couldn't tell you how I learned it.

It's just what we do.

I later discovered that grass can actually seed itself if you let it. It grows long, it looks bad, you may get an ordinance violation from your town, landscapers will frequently leave their business cards in your mailbox, and your neighbors will hate you.

One day my friendly octogenarian neighbor actually asked if my lawnmower was broken.

"Nope, all good here!" I replied. "Just running a little experiment."

A lawn left alone to naturally grow looks bad and the peer pressure to fix it immediately kicks in, but it will reseed itself. Take that, lawncare people!

Remember that conversation about maintenance?

Just another mere conjecture of mine in a book full of nonsensical musings, but doesn't it strike you as odd that you have to so arduously maintain the supposedly natural part of your property?

I presume that instead of seeing lawn maintenance as the pain in the ass that it actually is, our work-obsessed culture preferably views it as another way to have something annoying yet also obligatory to work on at home that conveniently shields us from quality time with our loved ones.

We shall call it *Turf Management.*

It sounds important, so don't question it and don't bother me while I'm busy doing yard work.

We may feel differently once the grocery store runs out of food and we realize we can't eat that grassy knoll we so delicately cared for all those years. That lawn on which we dump liters of water to create a safe space for the human foot and a pleasing sight for human eyes.

We are persuaded into using precious time, energy, and resources to keep a lawn alive instead of growing something that keeps *us* alive.

I can't wait to see how this one plays out.

[Edible] gardens

I commend those that exert the effort to start a home garden, but I'm an equal opportunity criticizer so the praise stops there.

Why is that garden locked down more securely than that fort that [allegedly] has all that gold?

Metal containers.

Fences.

Locks.

Mesh coverings.

Barbed wire?

Armed guard?

Land mines?

I suppose since gold is inedible you could make the argument that the contents of your garden are more valuable than what is [allegedly] out there in Kentucky, but if what's in your garden is that valuable, why do you allocate such a small percentage of your property for the purpose?

Nearly 95% of our yards remain useless while we grow food on the tiny remainder that we then lock down.

That's *our* garden, where we grow *our* food. No one else's. Back off!

If you think that last little rant sounded like a toddler — Yes.

Our problem-solving brains enhance our garden security while conveniently glossing over the root cause of garden raids. That teensy-weensy tiny detail that we transitioned all of kingdom-fucking-come from animal grazing and hunting lands into shopping malls and warehouses.

Animals aren't intruders.

They aren't carrying a personal vendetta against us and our private food stash that we deem so valuable that we only devote a small corner of our property to it.

We are not that important. No single human being ever is.

That deer is just fucking *hungry*.

Groundhogs don't have grocery stores. My little groundhog friends under my deck don't raid my garden out of malice.

They are just *hungry*.

The chipmunks don't eat my tomatoes because they hate me, although their tendency to take a single bite out of every tomato in the yard is frustrating.

They are just *hungry*.

When my neighbor's chickens visit my yard, they don't peck away at my spinach leaves because they are greedy.

They are just *hungry*.

The moles attack my potatoes from below not because they like pissing me off.

They are just *hungry*.

That little baby bunny I saw nibbling on my kale the other day…was so freakin' cute that it could do no wrong. Chomp away, little guy! The garden is yours!

If what you are growing is so critical, then grow more of it.

Line the streets with it.

Take your garden fences down. Toss the raised beds. Remove the security. Increase the percentage of your yard dedicated to supporting life, and stop using chemicals that take life.

Fence less. Grow more.

That's what I did.

It's not my yard anyway. I'm merely a steward of the land that human laws say I own, and with that, I cordially invite my furry friends over for a meal.

I'll step back and let it all grow.

[Don't] bring out your dead

I was sorting through my grandmother's paper files the other day when I came across one of those official-looking legal documents with fancy script and esoteric words that no one understands, and the first paragraph included a line like this:

"Section F, Sub-division 14, Plot 42."

My first thought was that my grandmother must have land somewhere, which would be great since I heard somewhat recently that land has a monetary value.

Maybe we can sell it!

Nope. I merely found the paperwork for my grandfather's burial plot in the local cemetery. It seems we take our property rights to the grave, even in death refusing to relinquish our land claims.

But hey, at least we downsize.

Our uniquely human obsession with the overarching concept of death gets its own chapter later, but that fixation, plus a heavy reliance on cemeteries, directly impacts how we allocate land.

Cemeteries. Large swathes of land sub-divided into plots claimed by the deceased for eternity, with eloquent stones placed in orderly rows to let us know who is there.

Or who *was* there.

The open space in between grave markers is maintained similar to our residential yards. Meticulous green grass where nothing else can grow, and no one walks on it unless you are visiting someone who isn't actually there anymore.

I would personally advocate for that unorthodox process where we bury ourselves below a newly planted tree, replacing mined stone with a natural living organism as our headstone, but I am confident each tree would eventually be cut down to build a convenience store.

While in death we lock up our bodies in those lovely coffins and urns, in life we shield ourselves from death, the one inevitability in life.

Despite legends of magic elixirs, fountains of youth, and the extremely well-off attempting to reverse the aging process for themselves because they can't seem to find anything more selfless to do with all those fake money credits of theirs, death will eventually come for us all.

And 'us all' is a lot of fucking people right now.

As we all inevitably pass on, our sacrosanct customs and traditions dictate more land must be set aside for the practices we deem unchallengeable by the very use of that fun word.

Sacrosanct.

It is 'sacred' ground that can never be repurposed. We even claim these areas are haunted in an attempt to rationalize the lack of human presence there.

It is off-limits. Untouchable. Says who, though?

Think through the impact of such claims, as the entire planet could theoretically become one large cemetery a few millennia from now. I want to believe we'd alter our burial practices before we got to that point, but I'll hedge my bets and challenge the practice right now.

Why does my grandfather, who died nearly forty years ago, still have a physical fucking address?

Unintended consequences of land use

Who cares if we remake the face of the earth as we please?

Everything looks fine!

Nature is simply resilient, and has for the past four or five centuries calmly absorbed our BS like a champ, as we give no thought to the potential consequences of our behavior.

How much more do we think nature can absorb though?

We don't care. We are mostly unaware that there is even a problem because everything is in order within our *humanity bubble*, but this planet of ours is a complex, multi-dimensional, interconnected web of subsystems that the human brain struggles to comprehend, and everything looks fine to us because we can't grasp the systemic interconnectedness across space and time.

Our perception is skewed.

In that same half-millennium timespan where nature acted as a huge punching bag for our hooks and jabs, we've reset what normal looks like and separated ourselves so far from nature we don't even see the true outdoors anymore.

We mislead ourselves by baselessly assuming that the adverse consequences from our bulldozing should instantly show up at the same time as the positive expectations and outcomes that we set out to achieve by altering the land.

We can start shopping closer to home right when that new department store opens.

Wonderful!

No adverse consequences showed up when we cut the ribbon at the grand opening, so there must not be any.

Also wonderful!

Except our shortsighted, human-centric, and immediate check for detrimental impacts right at project completion will never capture the consequences that show up later, and we reject any further responsibility after that initial review.

We complete our closeout meeting and move on.

We are altering the world around us. That small four-hectare wedge of land near my home was full of trees last week, and now it's a cleared building site for our 74th senior care facility in town.

Thank goodness, just what we needed. You know who doesn't need that? The fox I saw desperately trying to get through the fence and back to its now destroyed den.

Humans changed the face of the earth at that location.

It is different now.

We are the most ambitious interior decorators this biosphere has ever known, but we don't alter our behavior because it takes time for the consequences to reveal themselves.

Nothing immediately happens if I dig a hole, pour oil into it, and cover it, so I assume I'm off the hook. That black gold came from the ground, so what's the big deal? I'm just returning it to the earth.

But the effects can be unknowable for some time. Bury oil in your yard often enough and you may find that nothing grows a year or two later, and the EPA has a few questions for you.

I just ran a random search query and the search engine I used informed me that it took 320 milliseconds to complete the search.

Wait, that looks like a botched transition. Fire your editor, Brian!

That transition was actually intentional. In a society interested in how many *milli*seconds it took for our web search (the action) to generate 3.5 *billion* direct and supposedly specific search results (the expected outcome), how could we — and why would we? — internally process the unexpected adverse future impacts of dumping oil on the ground today?

Our mission was to rid ourselves of old oil. Mission accomplished, time to move on.

We don't process abstract ideas like this too well, so here are a few more random examples to emphasize this point.

Solar panels

Let's start with solar panels!

A rather benign topic, I think, and a great concept in the eyes of most people, unless a solar company sales blitz is currently canvassing your neighborhood.

I certainly have no interest in procuring them for my home. My town requires that I install panels on my roof, and despite having power generation right above me, my home would somehow not have electricity if the power goes out.

I get the technical explanation; I'm just questioning the logic.

I want to power my home directly if I have to drill holes in my roof, not sell it back to the power company for a credit on my electric bill. None of this overcomplicated and inefficient 'powerplant-generated- electricity-waving-to-my-solar-generated-electricity-as-they-pass-each-   other-along-the-transmission-lines' ridiculousness.

Anyway, let's focus on ground-mounted solar panels, and think about how much of the earth we are covering with them. We've devised a clever way to intercept the sun's radiant energy and convert it to electrical energy for our use, and we aren't wasting any time.

Great.

Solar panels are a novel engineering solution to the humanity-centric problem of requiring more electricity, but is what we need all that juice for actually important?

That's debatable, but more importantly, what was that radiant energy doing before we put those solar panels in place? Before the panels blocked that energy from contacting the earth's surface and doing whatever it was originally doing?

What it had been doing for what may as well be considered all of eternity.

That energy was hitting the ground and going *somewhere*.

Doing *something*.

That energy wasn't just hanging out idly on the surface, waiting for humans to ingeniously capture and consume it to power our cell phones and devices and cars and all that fun stuff.

That energy wasn't just disappearing either, assuming that the good ol' conservation of energy theorem still holds.

I don't know what it did before, and neither do you, but chances are it was doing things that we can't comprehend, and we won't realize the consequence of disrupting that process for at least decades.

We cannot see with our eyes the radiant energy transferring to the surface and into the earth.

That's radiant energy for you — conveniently invisible to the naked eye.

That's humanity for you — assuming no change because there is nothing to see.

The systemic changes we introduce cause an intricate downstream consequence that we cannot 'math' into a comprehensible form, but we will see the outcome soon enough.

Or we won't.

We don't know.

All we can say with absolute certainty is that there hadn't been a solar panel there for a *very* long time, but now there is.

The cloud

Here we are at the pinnacle of human advancement, and we exist in a world where we replace real farms that could feed us with buildings that provide the computing power for us to manage *virtual* farms that enrich someone else.

Everything is in *the cloud* now, though, so it's all good as far as we can tell, either unaware or unwilling to acknowledge that *the cloud* simply means that physical hard drives are no longer in our homes. We assume no impact because we don't see new server racks added in our basement each time we add storage to our accounts.

Our data is not floating out there in the clouds. File storage didn't suddenly *not* require physical space.

A nice double-negative for my English teachers as well, but it emphasizes the point.

It's just stored *over there* now.

We removed physical space requirements from our immediate environment and happily relocated it *over there*, occupying land out of sight. It's actually worse now, in that our imaginary stuff is likely on multiple computers instead of just one. Oh, and all of our data requirements exponentially grew over the past five years with the fun things we can do now, plus we must keep an additional backup.

Always have a backup.

We see no monetary cost associated with our online activity because we pay with our data, which leads us to ignore the resource cost of our digital behavior. Firms also absolve themselves of the responsibility to monitor how consumers use their products. They conveniently and silently granted users the substantial responsibility of self-regulation, and they keep supplying capability as long as we keep demanding it.

Consumers simultaneously assume they wouldn't have access to the capability if it weren't appropriate to be used freely and liberally, errantly viewing a product's presence on the market as permission to use with impunity.

We even poorly prioritize electricity usage to support our device addictions. It wasn't economically viable to return a nuclear power plant to service until an investment firm started poking around looking to power their data centers.

Let's run through that last sentence one more time.

A nuclear power plant remained dormant for what I can assume was a few decades, and societally we couldn't justify turning it back on until we wanted more juice for AI. Nothing else could apparently justify unleashing the immense power of a dormant nuclear reactor.

Distracted by the incredible fact that the computing capability that once took up an entire room can now fit in our pocket, we turn a blind eye as we fill entire warehouse-sized buildings with computers to handle un-limited pictures, endless cat videos, and virtual farms on those handheld devices.

It's different now.

Our responsibility on our side of the *point of receipt* is simple. We spared ourselves the eyesore in our immediate environment because the giant room containing the computer hardware is now somewhere *over there*. 'Room' is really an understatement these days — the largest data center in the world is almost 1,000,000 square meters.

Quick conversion for you foot and inch users: it's fucking huge.

Once there were no data centers. Now they are everywhere. At one time our computing power was in the same room as us, but now it is not.

Something changed.

Mind your search, please.

Retention basins

Retention basins are those large pool-like areas that you typically see near newly developed areas that are always empty until a torrential rain rapidly fills them.

We designed them to capture any runoff after development, since we know there will be excess water when we block the usually permeable sur-face of the earth with the impermeable foundation for a large building and additional supporting concrete and asphalt for sidewalks and parking lots.

We wouldn't want our expensive new building to flood, so accounting for excess rainwater makes sense.

Since that water must go *somewhere*, we pulled out our handy math formulas, accounted for a volume of water and flow rate, added some other fancy variables, and dug a hole large enough to handle a few times more than the expected amount.

Can't forget that factor of safety!

A simple math problem, done and done. Sure, the ground still absorbs all of that water, and it'll eventually reach the same aquifer, but once again *something* has changed. The water was doing *something* when it was evenly absorbed across a wide area that is now a building site.

We can say with certainty that we changed the water flow, and we are aware that water does things as it transfers through the ground and eventually gets to an aquifer or wherever it goes, yet we downplay the impact since we see no immediate changes.

Look at me. I've gone from an engineer to a person who says: "Water does things" and "...wherever it goes."

Ignoring my less than eloquent delivery, those water molecules served a purpose when they were evenly absorbed across a wide area.

What, exactly, we don't know.

We can't know.

It can't be expressed mathematically, so we dismiss it as irrelevant. We solved the math problem we established for this scenario, satisfied a few government mandated regulations, and our new investment hasn't flooded, so great success all around.

Very nice.

But once more these actions create a problem we can't see yet, one that we don't know is coming, and we don't know when it'll surface, because remember, we aren't the only ones changing the surface of the earth.

Over there is doing the same thing.

A wide land mass was at one time evenly absorbing water and nutrients. Now we sealed off a significant portion of that same land mass and concentrated water absorption in fewer locations.

Coastlines

Real estate websites have a filter for identifying waterfront homes.

Everyone wants to live there, and judging by the prices of these properties relative to similar plots further inland, we can easily see for whom these locations are reserved.

 And they reserve them, alright.

Owned because of the immense amount of money certain individuals make, but also generally unoccupied because they are too busy earning the astronomical amount of money needed to own them in the first place.

Some countries love the concept of waterfront real estate so much that they make their own islands to create more coastline.

When we run out of dock space, we cut new channels further inland to give properties waterfront access. You can see this quite easily on a map where we cut human-made bulkheads with straight lines and sharp angles while natural coastlines flow more—you guessed it—naturally.

Despite my grumblings — and possibly a bit of envy — it's really just simple economics. Supply and demand and all that, so all good.

The bigger, non-economic concern going unnoticed is how we rigidly fixed in place what was for eons a dynamic, fluid border between water and land.

The problem, of course, is that earth's bodies of water missed the memo — water can't understand a deed either — and it keeps crashing into this newly established boundary that marks the edge of our *humanity bubble*.

Oceans naturally erode the shoreline, subtly shifting and altering it to its will, but we took our permanent marker and drew a very real line in the sand with boardwalks and infrastructure and buildings and docks and ports and homes and hotels and resorts and bulkheads and dunes.

We counter earth's assault with massive beach replenishment projects to keep the water at bay, allowing my state's many beach-town municipalities to generate their critical beach badge revenue.

Yeah, we pay for beaches here. We also pay to park before we get to the beach. It's awesome.

Referring back once more to our natural disaster talk, we are repeatedly astonished when Mother Nature comes barging in and destroys these fixed objects we planted right near the water, somehow shocked that the water level surged to a point that destroyed our things, when this is what's been happening since the dawn of time.

Smart enough to earn the money to buy that property right there on the water, but inexplicably unwilling to grasp that the earth haphazardly shifts boundaries and will submerge that waterfront home at any moment for no reason.

Then there is the impact of restricting waterfront access to strictly human use. Stacking the beach with fenced-in row homes right next to each other all the way down the coast, blocking the inland from the water. What natural, biological processes are we preventing with our rarely occupied walls of luxury?

I don't know. I *do* know it can't be nothing, and that we will see the consequences eventually. This species of ours never ceases to surprise me, and in the meantime we'll just keep building bigger things near and over the water since we lack any clear immediate evidence implying there's a problem.

We own the land, and the coastlines are our crown jewels of the real estate world. We claim that land and we defend it against any non-human invaders, like those pesky seagulls at the beach.

Pests, we call them, *sea* gulls that are shooed away from their rightful place near the *sea* by the other definitely not invasive species who outnumber the native gulls on the sand by a factor of 500 to 1.

As we claim the beaches and shorelines, we create yet another impenetrable barrier that restricts water and land access to others.

The oceans, meanwhile, bide their time, and with the rising and falling of the tides naturally shift the shorelines as they always have, not giving a shit about what we put in their way.

We'll see who wins this one as we continuously replenish the beach and rebuild, only for it to be washed away once more.

Spoiler alert: we don't win this one.

Riding the waves of abundance

So here we are.

The land is ours; we made a bunch of stuff with what the land freely offered us, and now we have a place to store all that stuff.

Lines have been drawn.

Borders established.

Walls built.

Kings crowned? Nah, too far. No one is *that* great, and we don't do that here.

We continuously dissect the physical landscape with new roads, buildings, and fences, creating ever smaller pockets of nature that we eventually transition into our *humanity bubble*. Vast open spaces severed by our creations that impede our ability to exist in nomadic fashion once again.

Indigenous tribes can freely roam — at least that's what we claim — provided they remain within government-prescribed borders, while gypsies are now the bane of our existence on vacation.

"What country do you belong to?"

A question that we expect every human to answer before sentinels allow us to cross over an arbitrary line on a map and into a new land, removing our ability to simply exist as a living, natural, free creature on this planet. Our passionate displays of citizenship are nothing more than an unconscious proclamation that we are perfectly cool with being owned by one of those 190 or so abstract organizational entities to which we pledge allegiance.

At one time merely shepherds of the land, harmoniously integrating with, and at most guiding the growth of, the natural world with minimal interaction as we freely roamed, we have since conquered our surroundings and established obstacles to unwanted movement.

We stripped the living canvas of the earth bare with paint thinner and replaced it with our perception of the world.

We cover the ground with buildings, blocking the subterranean layers of the earth from the open air.

We capture the sky within our buildings, segregating the sky and keeping that trapped air at a comfortable 20°C everywhere.

We erect barriers between our illegitimately claimed land areas — invalid as far as the natural world goes — to impede the flow of those annoying migratory animals.

Invaders, we call these poor beings, with the most boisterous among those name-callers seemingly forgetting that their ancestors made the same damn trip a few generations prior, but then also magically remembering that voyage when it comes time to establish a holiday in honor of those valiant adventures.

Grasping that fourth dimension of reality is tough for us — that additional dimension being *time*, at least as far as physics is concerned — especially when doing so could crush our flimsy narratives.

Getting lost in all that noise, though, is the disruption of countless ecological processes that we don't understand, and while the rest of the biosphere gets it and disagrees with our selfish behavior, we continue on our consumptive path.

If something is there we might as well take it because nobody is around to stop us, we clearly have no willpower whatsoever, and if we don't take it, someone else will.

Ever so slowly we assume control of the world and everything in it.

Pixel by pixel.

Cube by cube.

Voxel by voxel?

We incrementally indoctrinate small portions of the natural world into our *humanity bubble*, but the joke is on us, since Mother Nature never signed over land rights to us.

We take more than we need

If we plotted resource usage by species on a pie chart, humans would greedily claim all the slices. It wouldn't be worth drawing a fine line to collectively account for everyone else because their portion is basically non-existent relative to our massive consumption.

I hate pie charts, but I'll happily use one here since the visual is just a damn circle.

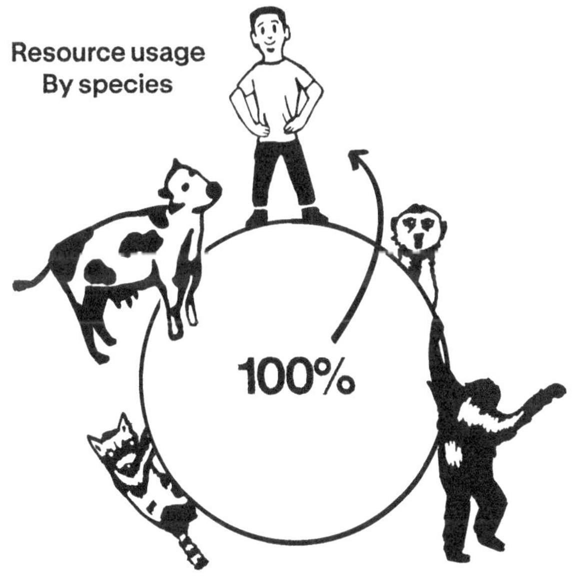

Possession is nine-tenths of the law, as the saying goes, but possession, and law for that matter, are both strictly human concepts.

We unilaterally decided everything around us should be owned — with no other species showing up for that discussion either — and when you establish the concept of possession, anything just laying around presumably becomes free game.

So, we take and we take, like the dominant toddler hoarding all the fun communal toys in their corner. We adeptly label such juvenile behavior as selfish, but we rebrand selfishness as initiative on our journey to adulthood. We love our things, we have way too many of them, and there are no balancing forces to guide what we take.

In theory we should be able to self-regulate by adulthood, but given the dozen or so self-storage units that only adults can rent within a six-kilometer radius of my home, I'd say we tossed those discipline lessons into the trash as we matured. I'll recklessly assume a non-trivial percentage of those units exclusively store seasonal holiday decorations, because nothing conveys true holiday spirit like a materialistic, income-generating social media post.

The illusion of abundance enables our excessive consumption today as we either completely refuse to believe, or ignore altogether, the simple truth that not wanting more is a perfectly acceptable, and for this planet preferable, state of being.

I refer you back to that pie chart that opened this chapter.

Find another species with stuff. Go ahead — I'll wait.

Despite the unsurprising revelation that we stand alone here, we must paradoxically acknowledge that we can't avoid having stuff right now.

My head may be in the clouds but my feet are firmly on the ground. The flywheel driving our economic machine is spinning too fast to simply jump off right now, and my retirement portfolio is heavily invested in everything propelling that flywheel's momentum, so for the sake of my long-term financial future I actually need us all to maintain the status quo for another few decades.

Keep buying, everyone!

I'm not even trying to apply a brake to that flywheel. What a mess that would be! We actually never built a brake into the system. Why would we ever need to throttle back in our *humanity bubble*?

I'm just conceptualizing what a brake could look like in 14 generations so we can start drawing the blueprints.

While we deliberate whether we should start the design process for that brake, we coast through life on autopilot, aimlessly purchasing things we don't need using this excess money that we so conveniently label *disposable* income, with each purchase having the same outcome as lighting that currency on fire.

Please enjoy your things — I genuinely mean that — but just remember that humans have stuff, while other species don't.

We always want new things

We find ourselves on a slippery slope of progress as we continue to take, create, and innovate. With pursuit of our primal needs long satisfied, we transition to desiring various wants, like wanting things we misperceive as needs, and wanting better, faster, more cost-effective ways to acquire our needs. Let's quickly review how our engineering brains permitted this transition in the housing, transportation, and entertainment worlds. Let's rejoin our trip through history and look at one potential theory on how we settled down:

- I am cold, but it's pretty warm near that forest fire that naturally started. Maybe we can create that ourselves?

- What if we created a shelter that we could stay in all the time? That would keep us safe from the elements.

- I want to see in the dark in that shelter that evolved into a house. Let's bring the fire inside!

- Shit, the house burned down. Maybe add a fireplace and chimney to contain that unpredictable chemical reaction?

- It's too smoky inside, even with the chimney we just built, so let's try some candles to help us see.

- My house burned down again because someone knocked the candles over. What else can we do? Here's electricity. Let there be light! And maybe let's also create a fire brigade since this fire stuff we insisted on harnessing really destroys stuff.

And then we got tired of staying put in one place:

- This landscape is boring. We should relocate. We'd better start walking.

- I want to go farther at a faster pace than my feet can take me, so I wonder if I could somehow ride that horse? It surely won't mind if I hop on its back and tell it where to go.

- Well, my horse can't cross that ocean, and I'm too impatient to wait for evolution to naturally make it possible. Better build a boat. Bring the horse too, in case we have to go far at our destination.

- My horse just died, and it was too slow anyway. One horsepower is so 17th century. Here's a train.

- That train is pretty nifty, but it has a pre-set path on tracks. I want my independence, and also some privacy. Here's a car and some roads that also require pre-set pathways.

- I want to take some of my stuff with me. Look, a bigger vehicle.

- Those boats from earlier are still too slow! Also, icebergs are dangerous, so have a plane.

- Let's fly around in space! I'm a spaceman now!

And then we got bored and suddenly didn't want to move anymore, so we brought entertainment to where we settled:

- I *want* to ski even though there's no snow — I *need* to install snow-making machines.

- I *want* to ski and I live in the desert — I *need* to build an indoor artificial ski slope.

- I *want* those plants I saw on vacation in my backyard because they brought me joy — I *need* to ship them in!

- I also *want* to play ice hockey in the desert — I *need* to build an enclosed stadium.

- I *want* to play baseball in the desert as well — I *need* to build another enclosed stadium.

We are emboldened to achieve the impossible, again not questioning whether or not we *should* do something, but instead putting down our beers and loudly proclaiming "Challenge accepted!" at every turn, apparently determined to prove we can function in the desert or fly on wings that are not ours in places where our lungs do not function.

Nothing is impossible, but certain things are not sensible.

We can't have nice things

Our practical creations inevitably transition to novelty, or in some cases even become weaponized against us. Consider some of our other greatest feats that are no longer useful:

Mail. Mail was once an effective communication medium. Does anyone get anything useful in the mail these days? Not me, but I do receive plenty of coupons each week, and my car dealership really wants me to trade up to a newer model.

Telephone. The telephone was another milestone in human communication, as evidenced by the few dozen museums globally where you can learn about its history.

Riveting.

Then came the telemarketers. Does anyone need an extension on their car warranty?

I picked up a phone call from a random number the other day, and the caller read me my address, asked me how old my roof was, and then abruptly hung up once I answered.

I'm sure the information was useful in some way, but I couldn't figure it out.

I spent the next three days wondering what I did wrong, and even checked my financial accounts periodically, inexplicably concerned that this individual somehow found a way to steal my banking information now that they knew the age of my roof.

I'm pretty certain that my roof's age wasn't one of my security questions, but I've been wrong before.

Internet. The internet was revolutionary, and it connected the world to a wealth of information. It is now a black hole of vitriol that we use to manipulate and sabotage each other, or just do dumb things. No further need to elaborate here.

Okay, fine, one example.

Remember those intercity 'portals' — really just live-stream cameras — that cities set up as a way to instantly connect people across the world? What a great way to express our commitment to the global human community!

If you are wondering how that went, the operators hastily shut them down because a human in one city flashed the other city in what was likely the first ever intercontinental public human flashing event.

Law. This one is currently in transition as the line between legality and morality slowly collapses.

An honorable and noble concept intended to provide people with an opportunity to defend themselves, you can now do whatever you want while the lawsuits pile up and take forever to process, and people with ample means can take advantage of those who aren't as well off because the cost of an initial retainer dwarfs the gross monthly income of the most vulnerable.

Planes. A great means of expedited transport, but now aircraft fly around with banners letting us know the best hospital to go to. If I'm hurt enough to require a hospital visit, the best hospital is probably the closest one.

I don't need to learn that from my beach chair.

Boats. Another form of sensible transport, and an effective means to catch fish. Now my view from the beach also includes boats bobbing along the shoreline with large TV screens mounted on their hull, advertising the latest hard seltzer flavors.

I don't need to see that information from my beach chair either.

Every innovation along our societal timeline starts off great but eventually becomes obsolete thanks to all of our superior technology, descending into a state of novelty and eventually nuisance on its way out the door.

We waste more than we should

I love when it rains from the ground and the sky at the same time.

Despite it being five o'clock somewhere on this planet, I am by no means under the influence of anything — at this time, at least — so I make this puzzling statement with a clear mind. I simply witnessed another lawn sprinkler system running during a downpour.

Forgiving those rudimentary automated timers for failing to account for the weather, we will instead focus on how this scenario paints a playful picture of the simple ways we waste.

Waste, defined in simple terms, is basically anything being used carelessly, extravagantly, or to no purpose.

The cunning linguists who defined this word conveniently added that little open-ended caveat at the end there — '...to no purpose' — and we really capitalize.

Despite an endless selection of educational materials covering waste and efficiency in countless facets of human life, we do a pretty poor job preventing waste where it truly matters.

To us, it all has a purpose, and therefore cannot possibly be wasteful.

The Landfill Economy

Our economy is—well—it truly is something. Raving lunatics like me may claim it is even too ridiculous to describe.

I'm not going there, though.

I am certainly no economist, and every classically-trained and self-proclaimed economic expert on the planet will come out of the woodwork to eviscerate me for whatever I might say about their precious economy, the heart of our *humanity bubble*.

Fuck it.

The mere mention of the word 'economy' already sent the economist army's spidey-senses tingling, so here's what I think:

Our economy fills landfills.

This economy thing is responsible for the mass aggregation and subsequent reallocation of resources from across the globe to concentrated pockets within our *humanity bubble*. We use global supply chains to build our mostly useless stuff, we use those things, and then discard them into a landfill when we are done with them.

I say 'mostly useless' because I am an out-of-touch minimalist curmudgeon who hates all of the things, but next time you are stuck in a line at a store where you are likely already buying useless items anyway, take a peek at the random crap available for purchase on the shelves next to you in line.

If you're at home, go through a kid's room and you'll see some more random crap that will eventually be thrown away.

Our beloved recycling campaigns are mere placebos as we oddly skip the *Reduce* part that opens our fun little "3 R's" jingle. Even the *Reuse* "R" gets a pass these days since it is not worth the time and effort to repair things. Somehow the part I need for my two-year-old vacuum costs more than an entirely new vacuum because the company has put out seven new models since I bought mine.

I don't recall any other species having generated waste aside from what comes out of their bodies, and that hardly requires a landfill.

You know what there *isn't* a search filter for on real estate websites?

Property close to landfills.

If there is, it's intended to help avoid being within smelling distance of these abominations we happily create but vehemently reject.

If each of us had our own personal mini-landfill right in our backyards, we'd be more selective, but since the big landfill is somewhere *over there*, our backyard can become a beautiful, pristine landscape with exotic plants, a pool, and a full outdoor kitchen. We remove our trash each week and never see the cumulative effects.

Food

If a universal translator existed and we told our fellow animal friends how we handle food, they would all murder us.

We are the worst with our food. Buffets, all-inclusives, warehouse stores, extra super-duper portion sizes, family size, bulk purchases.

All those excessive options exist in our bubble.

It may appear as free to you, but we all pay for that indulgence in some way thanks to the intricate infrastructure amassing behind the *point of receipt*.

We also feel no obligation to clear our plates, so to speak, thanks to that false sense of abundance we perpetuate throughout our lives.

The tops of strawberries are edible, but I suppose those leafy greens up there don't taste great in chocolate. I receive puzzled looks when I eat a carrot without skinning it, and I also consume the greens at the top. The looks I catch are even more amusing when I eat a kiwi that still has the fuzzy skin on it.

And let's not forget the ultimate no-no: eating something that fell on the floor.

Everything I just mentioned is actually edible, but someone just decided it was weird to eat it and we now throw it in the trash.

Random Acts of Wasteful

Let's walk through a few random and unorthodox examples of waste I've observed in my mundane and otherwise uneventful life so far.

Energy-Efficient Home Appliances

When net energy consumption actually *increases* despite introducing energy efficient products meant to decrease energy waste, we have a bit of a paradox, and someone named Jevon now has their name attached to the term.

Jevon's Paradox.

In essence, the light bulb that uses a fraction of the energy as its predecessor is great, but we're actually using more energy than before because instead of one inefficient bulb we now have 56 efficient ones.

We light up everything now because the efficiency gain gives us the false perception that we can illuminate the world.

High hats.

Accent lights.

Spotlights.

Outdoor lighting.

Mood lighting.

Closet lighting.

Under-soffit lighting.

Under-cabinet lighting.

In-cabinet lighting.

We light it all up.

Televisions are also more efficient and use much less power than ever before, but households of days past only had a single TV, typically in the living room.

Now we have them in every bedroom, the kitchen, in some cases embedded into our refrigerators, outside under our cabanas, and down in the basement. Some sports fanatics actually have multiple TVs on a single wall. There is an entire wall at a tennis stadium that has a series of tiny impact-resistant LED screens, creating a single 20- meter-long TV screen out of what was once a static non-powered backstop that can now show a bunch of flashy animations during player introductions.

We find ourselves in a similar situation with our computer monitors. I am happy to have a lower energy monitor available, but where we once had a single monitor, we now use six with our desktop computer, plus we have a laptop and maybe a few tablets and a cell phone or seven to go along with it all.

Refrigerators? Very efficient these days, but now instead of one we have four: in the kitchen, the basement, the garage, and outside by the cabana near the TV out there. Not to mention the wine cooler that is the size of that one single household fridge of yester-year.

We are poor stewards of energy with the improvements we make, refusing to bank the savings as we interpret the resulting energy efficiency as permission to stop monitoring our usage.

Home Renovating

I'm not spending a dime to improve my home before I sell it because the buyer will gut it regardless of its current condition. I maintain a clean house, but I just see the dumpsters out in front of every home that has recently sold and know better than to waste my time.

We want what we want, so we find the foundation we like that can support our vision in a desirable neighborhood hopefully away from landfills and maybe near water, then we gut the rest of the house and bring our vision into reality. Perfectly functional and in some cases brand new appliances and building materials end up in dumpsters during home renovations, and those dumpsters get emptied in—yup—landfills.

All because it was the wrong color or style or didn't fit the fung-schway (Feng Shui?) of our desired aesthetic.

Uncompromising in what we want, adamant that we deserve it, and refusing to settle for what already exists in its current form, we flush those fake video game credits that we call money down one of our five toilets to achieve our vision because we just don't know what else to do with all of that capital.

Grass Heating

You read that right; it says *grass* and not *gas*.

During one of those slow pre-game moments during a playoff game where producers need to fill time — there can never be idle time in our programming — a report showed how underneath an [American] football stadium there are a series of heating systems to prevent the field from freezing.

I thought that was fun, learning that the field ... has a *heater*?

Not the stands, the seats, or the club boxes. The field itself is heated.

Those without heat in that town staring at that stadium are probably okay with that, right?

Jet Fuel for Joy Rides

Continuing along with my overt vendetta against the sport with the wrong name, a final American football game recently began with how all major American sports events typically begin: a military flyover to close out the singing of the national anthem.

National pride. No objections.

Multiple military aircraft flew over the stadium at an exorbitant cost per flight hour, hopefully paid for by the sports league and not our tax dollars. I can personally think of better ways to expend those resources, but I am not presently challenging the tradition itself.

My particular grievance is that this finale took place *in a dome*.

Aircraft flew over an enclosed stadium and participants just watched the flyover footage on nauseatingly large stadium TV screens that sports fans of 50 years ago could never fathom.

Then we have our more recent ventures into the next echelon of the atmosphere, that whole commercial space travel thing.

Seems pretty cool.

Would I do it? Maybe.

Do I think the immense amount of resources needed to support such an endeavor could be put to better use? You bet.

Guard your resources carefully. We only get one planet.

We sabotage our essentials

Humans can presumably survive a few weeks without food, a day or two without water, and about five minutes without air.

We need these three essentials for our survival.

Period.

Not for comfort. Not because we like them. Not because an ad convinced us they would be fun to have.

We.

NEED.

Them.

Hopefully we can all agree?

We won't go into the exact timelines since they don't matter, and in the end that precise level of data would be irrelevant to my case.

If you still disagree, *[don't actually do this]* feel free to hold your breath and report back in ten minutes with an exact time *[don't actually do this]*.

Air remains free, abundant, and somewhat clean right now, so skipping that resource and recalling the other timeframes above, we can reasonably conclude that we are at any given moment about *two days* away from death.

Constantly being 48 hours away from death is pretty wild!

I am equally astounded by how we render unconsumable the readily available and abundant supplies of that very resource we require every few days. We get pretty pissed at our animals when they drop debris into their water bowls, and yet we gleefully pour poison into our global supply because we tell ourselves our drinking water can come from *over there*.

Let's pick on one prominent 19th century discovery for a moment — petroleum — and give some thought to what we may have done with that fun high-octane byproduct of the oil refining process before we called it gasoline. Where do you think that punchy petrol went before we realized it wasn't useless?

Here's a not-so-eyewitness account of how this probably went:

"Hmmm, what the hell is this clear stuff that came out along with my oil? What should I do with it? Well, it's a clear liquid. That liquid in the nearby river is [mostly] clear. I'll just dump it there."

It's clear-ish, and we're fairly simple-minded, so it probably just got dumped with the other clear liquids we know and see every day, such as a nearby river or stream. What a perfect waste removal tool, that water-based conveyor belt that removes waste and magically sends it *over there*, allowing us to completely forget about it and the corresponding impacts. Or we watered the grass with it, which would send it to an aquifer, from which we also drink.

Pure conjecture of course, but since that soon-to-be amazing hydrocarbon was not the main goal of the oil refining process in the early years and went unused for decades, we must have discarded it.

It had to end up *somewhere*. Likely in our water supply.

So, what could possibly possess us to destroy something we know keeps us alive?

Talk about a stupid question. It's very frustrating, especially since we *know* how important these essentials are, based on a quick look back at that whole subject of war.

We are well aware that these resources are essential because they are primary targets in our military campaigns. Think back on most wars in human history. All's fair in love and war, as the saying goes.

Raze the farms.

Destroy the granary.

Slay the livestock.

Dam the rivers.

Cut off the food and water supply.

Poison the food and water supply.

Lay siege to your enemies and starve them out.

Or suffocate them. Just make sure you have your gas mask on first.

Air.

Water.

Food.

These three resources are all that *truly* matter in life, but we inexplicably ignore their importance.

Other resources like lithium, cobalt, erbium, germanium, yttrium, nickel, samarium, cadmium, and promethium — our fire-conjuring titan friend gets an element, too! — are great for all the fun toys we make in our little play-world, but are useless for naturally sustaining life. They are actually pretty destructive, since we tear apart the landscape looking for them, but thankfully we dig *over there*.

You can't drink the acid in a car battery.

No one is clamoring to inhale the air from a smokestack.

Computer chips are amazing, but they aren't the snacking type.

So why are we downright careless with resources so critical to our survival? Three theories come to mind.

Wait. Four, actually.

The theory I almost forgot is relatively simple: We are the dumbest smart species on the planet. Too smart for our own good.

Now on to the next three.

Out of sight, out of mind

We disconnected from the natural world and connected to our *humanity bubble*.

Most of us no longer get our food or water directly from the earth. It comes from *over there*, likely processed and wrapped in packaging, and we are completely removed from the gathering process that occurred weeks before we clear the grocery store shelves. I was picking vegetables in the garden one day and my inquisitive child said to me:

"Daddy, why do we grow all these vegetables in our back yard when you can just buy them at the grocery store?"

There you have it, the human upbringing. We can't help it, of course. A perfectly valid question from a child who, until assisting me in the garden, learned from their surroundings that food is always packaged and originates from the store.

I'll go out on a limb and claim that virtually none of you reading this have ever slain their own cow for a steak. I personally wouldn't know where to start, and one look into a cow's innocent little eyes and I'd be like: "Nope! I'll eat some more kale. Live long and prosper, my bovine friend!"

While a lion cub instinctively stalks their sparse prey out on the savannah hoping for a meal, our offspring raid their pantry of manufactured foods at will, eating when they please.

Food is sold to us in grocery stores, which we buy with money.

Water is delivered to us through the tap, which we buy with money paid to our local municipal authority, or we buy bottles of it from the same grocery stores that sell our food.

At least air, for the moment anyway, remains the last holdout, until we eventually have to buy cans of air for breathing purposes like in that '80s era sci-fi spoof movie.

Look it up. *"They don't make comedies like they used to,"* says every generation ever.

There is no longer a need for us to work directly for that which keeps us alive because someone else gathers it and we buy it.

Our *point of receipt* is basically our doorstep, and we don't trace it beyond there. While we've chalked this delivery mechanism up as a win for humanity over simply relying on the natural world, are you honestly comfortable trusting such a complex system, one over which you have no control, with providing the essentials you need to live?

No *immediate* harm – no foul

The next theory involves that whole feedback thing again.

We're adding droplet-sized negative impacts into a liquid storage tank that has the same volume as the Pacific Ocean. The feedback lag is so long, and individual contributions appear so inconsequential, that we don't uncover the problem until we cross the tipping point and something breaks.

Remember that canned air reference I made to close out the last section? That movie is almost 40 years old at the time of this writing, and aside from a few close calls like the LA smog fiasco and the Beijing Olympics air quality issue, we've managed to avoid any significantly noticeable air-related catastrophes that this particular movie overtly attempts to foreshadow.

We assume no immediate consequence means no issue, ignoring nearly four decades worth of negative impact that has built up but just hasn't reared its ugly head yet. Don't worry though, we somehow very clearly understand and acknowledge how our retirement accounts can compound in the same timeframe using the same math.

Enjoy all that money.

Now, four decades is pretty solid as far as a scientific study goes, so it's easy to rationalize our behavior, since nothing bad has happened in such a 'long' timespan.

But our perception of time is also too human-centric.

Four decades is half a lifetime for a human these days, but a mere blip on a multi-*billion*-year-old planet. Divide 40 by two billion to calculate that percentage, and the number will be so small that your calculator will show a formula that is unrecognizable to most (hint: there's an "E" in it).

That may not even count as a blip – it's more like the blip's blip.

Our individual contributions silently amass over time, but our human sensors cannot process the incremental changes or the indirect effects of our collective actions over such expansive intervals. We would have more success weighing a hydrogen atom on a truck scale at the highway inspection station.

Things just don't change drastically enough over our lifetimes to notice, even though the storage tank is slowly reaching capacity. The earth is on a different scale, so impacts from the earth's perspective could realistically take centuries to register. We stubbornly apply a timescale of decades against events spanning eons, and seeing no visible change, assume all is well and proceed.

We take down that tree near us, but we can still breathe.

We put a big, beautiful building on our farm near us, but we still have food on our table.

We pollute a stream near us, but we still have drinking water coming out of the tap.

The detrimental outcomes of our actions could be decades away, but we'll remain oblivious until they are upon us. They take a very long time to surface, but if we're 99% of the way through the 'negative consequence' accumulation process, we may not acknowledge the buildup but we will sure as hell experience the inflection point.

Reliance on Past Performance

Past performance is no guarantee of future results.

Ick. I could barely force my fingers to type that line.

Are you familiar with this one? Another piece of investing advice that we would be wise to apply to our essentials.

We're confident that because that tap has always provided water, it will continue to do so for as long as we need it. We're confident the grocery store will always have food on the shelves when we go. Air will always be clean enough to safely breathe.

I would proactively label myself paranoid and spare you the trouble, but that whole pandemic thing of the early 2020s gave us a glimpse of what could happen to our food and water supplies without notice.

Another pandemic isn't likely — famous last words? — but we're one locked door away from not being able to access the grocery store, and simply breaking in only sustains us until the existing stock runs out.

Our water was undrinkable for weeks that one winter I mentioned earlier where our town oversalted the roads. Compare that timeline to our 48-hour requirement for water.

Food and water have been abundantly available long enough for us to safely assume their consistent, perpetual presence in our lives, and therefore we don't need to worry about them. We have ingrained in ourselves the unsubstantiated notion that stable access to our three lifelines over generations in the past guarantees they will always magically appear from *over there* moving forward and we won't have to worry.

We can focus our attention on extracting and harvesting those other rare earth minerals to make what we *want*, because availability of the essentials we *need* is a sure bet for us.

A seemingly sensible thought process taught to us since childhood, but we'll end my doomsday pontificating with two questions that are worth mulling over in your minds:

1. Can you honestly guarantee for yourself and your loved ones that these essentials will always be there?

2. What would you do if those essentials weren't there one day?

This line you are reading right now is here for the sole purpose of not ending this section with a list. You aren't supposed to do that, and I've broken enough writing rules already.

Remember the basics

We depend upon the air, water, and soil on this earth to keep us alive.

We require nutrients from the soil to grow edible plants for us, and for certain animal friends of ours to consume before we eat them.

We require clean water, and the minerals naturally added to that liquid by springs and rivers that our refinement processes remove.

And we require fresh, breathable air, preferably without all the toxins from our various manufacturing processes and vehicles.

We are no different than our precious cell phones, untethered and free but running on stored energy that needs daily recharging for optimal function. We just tend to recharge our bodies with dirty power most of the time.

Unbeknownst to us, we've tipped the scales past the point of harmony. We are feverishly consuming Mother Earth's bounty, and we are outpacing her ability to sustain us.

It actually appears that she is low-key quiet-quitting on us.

We arduously pry our essentials from Mother Nature

Step outside right now and find food.

Simple enough, right?

You cannot go to a grocery store or the fast-food joint on the corner. For the moment, also forget the garden you may have in the backyard, since that is technically *humanity bubble* property.

Just step outside and eat something.

Anything.

Find something growing naturally out there and just eat it.

Pick plant leaves.

Kill an animal.

Grab a few mushrooms if you know which ones are edible.

Any luck?

What about a water source? Find a naturally occurring freshwater source from which you are willing to drink without filtration.

How'd that go?

Not well, I would guess.

Nothing readily grows around us, there are no crystal clear springs or streams near us, and you can barely find any animals in your area that you'd want to hunt. Even if sufficient wildlife were present, how would you hunt them? There's no app for that, and we won't put in the time and effort to learn the old-fashioned way because we're all too busy hunting virtual monsters across town using our phones.

Fun collaborative game? Or the easiest intelligence-gathering gimmick in the history of the world?

We'll never know.

We'll take a small win for now and celebrate that we don't need to breathe air out of a can, but we should probably give some thought to why two of our three essentials are not readily abundant and available to us at any given moment. That seems like a pretty clear sign that the earth has given up on trying to sustain us.

Unfortunately, us humans — men in particular — are typically clueless when facing such obvious signals, and I am guilty as charged.

Maybe?

Sorry, I wasn't paying attention. What am I owning up to this time?

This billboard is tough to miss, though, and while my eyesight is terrible these days and I may be misinterpreting what I see, I can vaguely make out Mother Nature flipping both middle fingers our way. A subtle, passive-aggressive proclamation on a big-ass road sign that we are on our own. We ignore the 'Slow Down – Road Out' sign in the distance and merrily skip along our societally accepted path.

Any sustenance supply issue is a problem to be solved with a new solution, and none of the potential alternatives take into consideration what we could stop to solve the problem. There is no need to cease altering the land *right here*: let someone else keep growing food and bottling water *over there* and ship it in.

We're killing it with these bold strategies of ours.

In our immediate vicinity we prevent the natural growth of anything edible and treat our water supplies ~~like~~ with garbage. I started writing a simile here but then I remembered that we legitimately dump our garbage into waterways.

Ever the stubborn industrious species, we take it upon ourselves to fix our sustenance problems by implementing a better way.

Gardening sucks...

Unfortunately, that better way of ours, farming and gardening, is a pain in the ass. Two green thumbs way down, as anyone who has ever tried gardening knows the struggle.

Balanced soil nutrients.

Sufficient water levels.

Proper temperature regulation.

Ample sunlight.

Minimal pests.

Sometimes it is impossible to pull edible foods from the soil, like you are in a tug-of-war with someone on the opposite side of the earth.

My claim of starting a re-wilding project at my house is actually a cover for giving up on this whole gardening thing and letting my entire yard grow as nature intended. I tried our fancy agricultural methods, but at this point if the earth can't naturally provide for me, I'll just exit stage right and the groundhogs can have my house.

I'll leave the deed on the back porch.

Thanks to that relatively short-sighted decision of our distant ancestors to turn agrarian some myriad years ago — it's so awkward using myriad like this! — here we are, reliant on agriculture as our primary means of sustenance for the majority of the human population. We must either intentionally grow the food we eat, or grow food that we feed to the animals that we eat.

I'm sure each successive generation felt they were on the right path, a logical progression of numerous milestones along our evolutionary timeline. I don't blame our ancestors, but when you consider that our multi-million-year-old genus — the *Homo* part of *Homo sapiens* — has only been doing this farming thing for around 10,000 years, we can't really claim a W yet.

We collectively fail to look ahead well, and our unprecedented access to food negates any need to evaluate our current eating practices.

Our path has, in a short period, taken us from eating unprocessed food and meat directly from the land in our immediate vicinity, to consumers hoarding food products on their shelves that concerningly last a year and 'cost-effectively' receiving grapes from South Africa and steaks from Australia here in the US.

The immense difficulties we experience growing our own food probably explains why no other species farms. If I were any other species watching this *Homo sapiens* shit show of an experiment unfold, I sure wouldn't attempt to garden. Humor me for a moment and visualize a gopher wielding a hoe.

Other species need none of it, and there isn't much to their strategy.

If they are hungry, they go off and find something to eat.

If they are thirsty, they find a puddle or stream or overturned contractor bucket with a thin film of water on it from which they quench their thirst.

No choice, no selection, no variety. Just eat and drink what is there. If it's not there, move to where it is available.

If you fail, you die.

Perhaps the most ingenious move by all those other species that smarty-pants humanity deems stupid is cleverly allowing humans to put extraneous effort into cultivating edible foods and then raiding their harvest. They are just hungry, but they sure aren't dumb if they are exerting the least amount of effort possible to nourish themselves.

Even with the immense amount of land we develop and render unusable, other species still fill their bellies enough to survive.

Cows eat grass.

Rabbits eat clover.

Foxes eat rabbits.

Groundhogs eat my kale.

Birds eat seeds.

Deer eat my hostas.

We easily say that our intellectual superiority is the reason why we are the only ones who do things like garden, but that's exactly how a superior species would rationalize their own odd behavior, stubbornly defending their better way from criticism as they push out of balance with the rest of the world, unwilling to even contemplate a shift back to how other living creatures naturally obtain their essentials.

We are no more than the co-dependent, high-maintenance significant other of the species world. Very particular, extremely demanding, never satisfied, and about to be dumped by our primary caretaker.

We require a vastly complex infrastructure to feed us in our *humanity bubble,* relative to what other species require to survive, and the logistics system we put in place for our essentials is simultaneously a modern marvel and a convoluted nightmare.

Take a moment to actually contemplate the byzantine food generation process we built beyond the *point of receipt* in our vain attempt to one-up nature:

Fertilizer.

Feed.

Pesticides.

Human labor.

Farm equipment.

Manufacturing facilities.

Shareholder meetings.

Government requirements.

Resource pricing formulas.

Purchasing contracts.

Delivery routes and schedules.

Grocery stores.

Delivery trucks.

Refrigerators.

Vehicles with enough room for groceries in the back.

We take basic, truly natural ingredients, ship them to factories across the world, mash them all together, and then mix in chemicals and flavors that in most cases concerningly double as fragrances for air fresheners and toilet bowl cleaners. Oh, and bonus points for using those other chemicals that make the food product last a long time on the shelf, in case we don't want something right away.

Companies then ship completed food products to a grocery store where we drive in a car to buy the stuff, or more recently we've evolved to the point where we can simply open an app, select what we want, and it magically appears on our doorstep.

Once the food is in our home we prepare a meal and then it's finally time to eat.

For a bunch of optimizers and expert problem solvers, we sure dropped the ball on feeding ourselves efficiently.

Somehow convinced that the value of next day delivery, rental properties, and unlimited cloud storage trumps feeding ourselves, we consequently removed ourselves so far from the source of our essentials that we'll never be able to tell if there is an issue. We cannot buy essentials off the shelf if there are no essentials left in the store, and we'll never know when that happens until we're standing there staring at empty shelves.

Here comes that feedback lag!

By the time we see the store shelves empty in such a hypothetical scenario, the base ingredients have long since dried up. The moment we see an empty shelf isn't the moment we run out of food. We ran out long before that and we just finally used up the existing inventory.

I suppose this system provides a benefit to *certain* people, though, as our *humanity bubble* demands a different type of efficiency.

We take comfort in the consistency with which food is available, absolving ourselves of the obligation to think through its origin. We confidently ignore our food system because it just works.

What a world.

A world where we walk outside and see nothing to eat because we strayed so far from the biosphere's natural equilibrium that we must now coax food out of the ground to stay alive.

We foolishly ceded direct control of keeping ourselves alive to third parties, and Mother Nature is subtly informing us that we are on our own, so we did the sensible thing: screamed "Hold our beers" and flipped our middle fingers back at Mother Nature again, and smashed our foot down on the accelerator.

Quick PSA: Don't drink and drive, folks.

I'd like to say we are being successful, but I understand we are facing a pretty dire topsoil situation in this century.

But hey, who needs dirt anyway? That stuff is so unclean.

...So does our water

Water was once abundant.

Sorry, let me rephrase. *Potable* water was once abundant.

I've seen the Hudson. Plenty of water there, but I'm not dipping a straw in that one. The fumes off the water would probably disintegrate the straw before it hit the water line.

We polluted our drinking water in pursuit of innovation, at which point innovation was then put to work making water drinkable again.

I had well water at my childhood home, and at some point in the '90s the well source became polluted — thank you, local superfund site! — so we were given access to *city water*, as we called it. A water meter hooked up to our house with a dial that charged us by the unit as we consumed water.

Whatever the hell a unit is.

Now we can't even drink that city water right out of that tap — we need to filter that too.

Let's follow that thread.

In a matter of decades, I personally went from drinking water right out of the ground from a well to filtering supposedly already filtered water supplied by an organization that prides itself on filtering water for a living. Does that seem like a good direction to be heading with that resource we can barely go a day or two without?

We can arrogantly claim that it's simply a sign that certain water is not up to our standards, but the more realistic scenario is that we are picky, sensitive drinkers. Extrapolate that problem out a millennium or two and think of the effects on every picky species on this planet.

That's just us, by the way. We're the only picky ones.

We would sooner ship water in from across the ocean, sometimes from as far away as a tiny Pacific island or the mountains of another continent, than clean up our act at home. Those poor locals on that island probably thought they were safe due to their isolation.

Think again. We destroyed our local water supply so we could have toys, and now we're here for your water!

We find it more convenient (READ: cost-effective) to fly water across the globe than to simply care for our own local water sources right at our feet, which I suppose makes sense.

Destroy the nearby water supply badly enough, and yes, the cost of remediation will be huge compared to flying in a few pallets of water.

Well played.

Let's help her along

Our species has developed quite a few unacknowledged Achilles' heels as we relinquished our ability to directly keep ourselves alive. Consider how screwed we would be if cows, pigs, and chickens suddenly took a permanent leave of absence.

We fail to make that connection, however, because we can always find that package of meat on the grocery store shelves.

It's always just there.

Our food friends don't get vacation time. We contain them, tag them, and track them all the way to the slaughterhouse, guaranteeing a steady meat supply by keeping enough inventory on hand in the fridge, on a farm, or on a freshly cleared section of that forest that is also the lungs of the earth.

Insert a periodic reminder of how COVID challenged our otherwise secure food supply assumptions. Past performance, and all that.

Other species find their food out in the natural world. They don't have an issue; they just apply the majority of their energy and effort directly to that purpose.

That stupid inferior squirrel has no problem finding a nut every once in a while without going to a store, and our consistent destruction of the landscape strengthens the resilience of that squirrel and all its friends in nature as we increase our dependence on our *humanity bubble*.

That's clearly a long-term disaster, but irrelevant to a species that thinks about things three months at a time.

As long as there is an app that delivers food right to our door, we don't need to hunt. Eating is no longer the direct outcome of the work we do now, as we rely on a complex artificial subsystem to provide us with our needs in exchange for currency.

If there ever were a long-term indicator that our time is limited, the fact that the natural world does not provide sustenance for the human race would be a prime contender.

As the earth withholds from us, we demand its subservience as we pump the surface of this rock with the equivalent of steroids. The earth reluctantly obliges, but with Mother Nature being the stubborn one that she is, there could be a good reason she no longer bountifully provides for us.

In a world where we readily accept the term 'it comes naturally' as a way to express things that are simple and require no exhaustive effort, the fact that our food does not come to us naturally is rather 'sus' as the young ones are saying these days.

A quick pause for all the Gen Z and younger peeps to cringe at the millennial as he tries to stay hip and relevant.

Leave nature alone to do what she naturally does best. She may not provide the riches we've come to desire, but she'll easily provide everything we need to keep us walking this earth.

That sounds like a reasonable offer.

Our Relationship with Other Species

We categorize our friends

So, it appears we treat the planet like shit. Nice job, everyone. How are we doing with our fellow species?

Not better.

A quick peek at the very first page of a certain religious text that some humans swear by explains our collective stance pretty clearly.

"Let us make man in our image, after our likeness. And let them have dominion over the fish of the sea and over the birds of the heavens and over the livestock and over all the earth and over every creeping thing that creeps on the earth."

Genesis 1:26

Other species missed the open comment period for signing their rights away to us.

We will gloss over the questionable legitimacy of a book written by humans declaring that humans get to run the world and focus on that word *dominion*.

When we consider the era in which this passage was written, *dominion* refers more or less to the authority and responsibility to govern, manage, and steward something. The original intent appears as a directive to *take care* of our fellow species and coexist with them on this rock that under normal circumstances has plenty of everything for everyone, but our modern interpretation took on a more aggressive and controlling stance.

We definitely missed that memo, and individual treatment of any particular species hinges on the value it brings to us in our *humanity bubble*. We like order and we like labels, so we subconsciously categorized our nonhuman neighbors based on their perceived usefulness and aligned them to a weird Maslow-esque hierarchy:

1. Sustenance.

2. Clothing.

3. Companionship.

4. Entertainment.

5. Experimentation.

6. To be Determined.

----

7. ~~Predators.~~

Here's the reader's digest version if you're in a rush: If we can't eat it (1), wear it (2), snuggle it (3), cage it (4), or test shit on it (5), then we don't care about it, but we'll keep a detailed record of it in case we figure out a use for it later (6). If a species fell into the 'negative usefulness' area below that horizontal line, say any of our predators that could kill us, we neutralized it (7).

For those that have a bit of extra time, let's begin our more detailed conversation with the most valuable species category in our hierarchy: those that support human nourishment.

Sustenance

We have to eat.

Some human diets include meat.

Some do not.

Whatever works for you, I just kindly ask that the meat you consume comes from a different species.

Current dietary trends notwithstanding, we were once great hunters. Then nothing hunted us anymore, so we settled down, fenced in what we once hunted, and kicked up our feet.

The closest we come to a hunt these days happens when we mercilessly fight each other for shiny new toys during the holiday shopping season, or when we seek out the last package of meat on the grocery store shelves during a pandemic.

Hunting dogs, now without purpose, have been demoted a few levels in our eyes to mere best friends of ours.

We made life easy on ourselves by breeding the animals we ate most — breeding of course being that fun word we use for "farming living things that are not connected to the earth" — and found ways to control other animals that could help us grow our plant-based food.

Let's have a look at this perfect subsystem of ours by starting in the most obvious of places.

With oxen, of course.

Animals at work

What an odd starting point: oxen. I'm an odd one, what can I say?

Our treatment of this animal in particular piqued my interest. Historical evidence is probably sparse — I didn't really look — so I'll venture an educated guess and assume the thought process went something like this:

"Well, we can't milk it, but we could eat it... Hmmm. It's pretty strong, and I am *le tired*. Got it. Let's put it to work, and then we'll eat it once it can no longer work!"

That's a pretty shitty retirement from a job that those oxen probably didn't want to do in the first place. Did we ask if they were okay with such a piss-poor retirement plan of immediate death?

Did we ask that ox if it was okay with us completely upending its routine that day when we first decided to put it to work?

Of course not, that would be foolish. Also, please don't talk to animals, at least not in this context, as that would be crazy.

We laugh at such absurdity, but internally we know the truth. We would belligerently tell someone to go to hell if they started strapping us up and telling us where to go throughout most of the day.

Again, pure speculation. I don't know, maybe some of you are into that kind of thing.

You do you.

Those oxen actually did try to tell us to go to hell. They're pretty freaking strong, apparently, which would explain why we wanted to put them to work in the first place, so we did the sensible thing.

No, silly reader, we didn't come to our senses and let them be.

We castrated them.

For the uninformed, that term *castrate* is fun terminology for slicing off their testicles to reduce testosterone production, rendering them nice and docile.

The plight of these creatures represents at least one scenario where we start implementing devices like harnesses.

And collars.

And leashes.

And bridles (not to be confused with bridal).

Who decided it was a bright idea to restrain another living creature around the neck?

By now we've replaced most working animals with machines in a decent portion of the developed world, relieving most animals of the duty they not-so-willingly accepted from us. They now await their next human-dictated assignment in that *To Be Determined* category that we'll talk about in a bit.

Our transition into factory farming

Other species await a different fate behind a fence.

In addition to using animals as labor to farm our plant-based food as we settled down, we also transitioned to farming animals for food. I want to believe that we sent oxen back to that *TBD* category to live long enjoyable lives, but we probably just skipped right to their retirement.

That would be the 'killing and eating them' part.

I won't venture to guess how we landed on steak, pork, and poultry as our 'big three' for meat consumption. That's the meat of cows, pigs, and chickens for those tracking the terminology game. I'll just assume there was more trial and error and move on to highlight the relationship between our laziness and the level of freedom and fair treatment of the animals we eat.

We started by hunting freely-roaming animals, but we penned them in with a fence as we started claiming property so we didn't have to chase them too far. True to our optimization habits, we increased the number of animals per square meter of that pen, reducing our workload and increasing occupant density similar to how commercial airline seating in coach gets progressively smaller over time.

A few centimeters at a time, and no one will notice.

Observing in nature how little space these animals occupy, we apparently assume they'll be okay actually being enclosed in that volume, with no more than a few cm^3 larger than the volume of their bodies to exist, and being grown for the sole purpose of being killed so another species could eat you.

Adding insult to injury, the individual doing the killing isn't even the one eating you.

How weird.

Desensitized by nebulous terms, we completely dissociate the steak on our plate from the once-living cow that made our meal possible, making this process easy to stomach by removing ourselves from that gruesome harvesting part that now resides on the other side of the *point of receipt.*

No need to look the cow you are about to eat in the eyes when you're merely picking up a plastic-wrapped tray of red meat.

Should all of us eat meat?

Maybe.

Maybe not.

That decision is more of a personal choice, and since I am no dietician I'll leave that to you and your team of experts to decide.

If I had to guess, there are probably a few people that legitimately can't eat meat for health reasons. Some could possibly have a bit more than they currently consume, while most eat more than their fill. I make that last judgement based on the skyrocketing meat consumption trend over the last century, and the corresponding recommended increase in protein intake.

I think my schooling may have indicated something about us being om-nivores — it didn't come up in a math class so I wasn't fully paying at-tention — but true to my goal of harmony I'll conclude by saying the best consumption approach is probably a simpler, more balanced diet of mostly raw and unprocessed foods.

A diet that lacks a succinct title that haters could ignorantly and effortlessly berate.

We close with a subtle reminder that most of us eat what once was a living creature; in most cases we did absolutely nothing to directly contribute to the hunting and subsequent processing of that creature into an edible form, and we would probably starve to death if we needed to procure it on our own.

Where did the terms poultry, beef, and pork even originate? I'm not sure, but we are desensitized to the point where we process species similar to how we mass produce smartphones, and we trade animals on commodities markets the same way we trade copper or cotton.

The fate of these three species is just a math problem at this point. How many of them can we keep alive and fatten up in close quarters to ensure we meet our tremendous meat wants?

Wants.

Not needs.

We have gone from dominion to domination in a few short millennia, two words with similar roots but drastically different implications.

Treat our animal friends kindly, and consume them wisely.

Clothing

The fire we mentioned earlier can go mobile for lighting purposes, as we've seen in countless movies involving a torch conveniently waiting for our brave protagonist at the perfect moment every time.

Has anyone in the last century actually done that, by the way?

This portable light source doesn't provide us with much heat though, so we found ourselves using the fur of the animals we already killed for food to keep us warm when we strayed away from our fire.

That seemed like a great idea back then, but fast-forward a hundred thousand centuries and our relentless pursuit of comfort has threatened our ability to survive in our own skin. I suppose that's why we resorted to hunting various animals over the centuries for their hides, as the term 'Fur Trade' rings a faint bell in my memory banks right now.

Nothing like bartering for the skinned remains of a once living creature.

We reject our body's natural attempts to keep ourselves warm because we believe hair is bad, and somewhere along the line we decided to wage war on any sign of hair growing on our bodies. Surely we have all noticed that humans are the only species requiring such extensive artificial or unnatural body coverings to survive:

- We get frostbite if our bare skin is exposed to the cold.

- Our skin burns when excessively exposed to the sun.

- Insects bite us like crazy when they find exposed skin.

- We cry when we step on something while barefoot (those little plastic building blocks are a killer!).

What other species require being handled so gingerly?

You'll find no cushioned sneakers on a jaguar. Their feet naturally developed protection and even the runt of their species easily outruns our fastest human sprinter.

Bears don't need cozy blankets. They have all the fur and fat they need to stay warm.

You won't find birds wearing cute little raincoats, as adorable as that would be to witness. They quickly grab their food and return to their shelter.

At least we have the biggest brain though.

So, we are weak. Got it. Now what?

Keep your pants on, folks. Don't mistake this section as a campaign for a global nudist colony. Do not go streaking down through the courtyard, the quad, or the gym. I see enough skin at the beach.

When I tell my partner to grow a beard like mine when she complains about her face being cold in the winter, it is just a joke. Don't propose that either, unless you're up for a boring, likely abstinent, winter.

This is a thought exercise.

Stripping away our clothing and allowing our random body hair to re-grow in this moment will not abruptly reverse millions of years of evolution. We won't suddenly grow a fur coat. Our efforts will fail, we will freeze, and we will make a fool of ourselves.

But if we want to survive another million years we should contemplate why we so vehemently fight this natural protective mechanism by donning artificial substitutes over our bodies.

Once nomadic and in sync with the natural world, we now insist on staying in places where we can easily become frostbitten or sunburned. Surviving in austere environments isn't easy, but we can live in them now thanks to our *humanity bubble*. We refuse to periodically move to places that are naturally comfortable because we simply feel entitled to staying in one place.

Throw us outside in the wild and we are screwed.

At least the snowbirds among us somewhat exhibit our primal behavior as they transition between north and south for summers and winters, but for the vast majority of us who haven't done our time and achieved the 'retirement life' checkpoint yet, we simply rely on our innovations to comfortably remain in places we shouldn't regularly inhabit to do things we cannot truly explain.

Fortunately, most of the animals that had absolutely no issue with unwillingly supplying their coats to us were eventually demoted to that *To Be Determined* category as plant-based and then synthetic clothing options took over.

Not out of kindness, mind you — natural growth was just too slow for us.

One last thing: dogs don't need coats. They need to remain in their natural habitat.

Dogs evolved to survive in their native environment, and if we moved them from that location to a place where they don't naturally exist, they'll probably be uncomfortable.

That's on us. They're just fine where they came from so leave them in their place.

"But the dog is shivering!"

Of course that Chihuahua is cold!

They are native to Mexico, that very warm, arid country down south with a state that shares the same name with that dog breed, so it most definitely will freeze when we bring them up north.

You don't see them walking up there on their own, do you? They stayed in place even when the boundary was unobstructed.

That Newfoundland is from — you guessed it — Newfoundland.

Canada.

They will be a bit hot in the south.

This should be obvious.

I intentionally selected dog breeds where their origin couldn't be clearer, but the concept applies to every animal. They evolved in certain locations before we interjected and rapidly moved them across the globe. Speaking of pets...

Companionship

Our bellies are full. Our bodies are warm. Time to fill our hearts!

If you want a quick chuckle, do what I did while proofreading just now and imagine hearing that last line in the voice of everyone's favorite animated snowman.

The frozen one, not the frosty one.

Few pets are officially registered as emotional support animals, but *any* animal you keep as a pet at home is an emotional support animal.

What other realistic purpose could keeping a pet possibly serve?

We absolutely loathe the mere thought of poop, so we wouldn't voluntarily clean up the waste of other species unless we were receiving something greater in return, which in this case is an emotional connection we can't seem to find elsewhere.

Pets comfort us, just like everything else in our bubble. They help us feel our feels, and those feelings can be positive or negative.

We cuddle them, and we get excited about seeing them when we come home, likely because we're just happy someone is happy to see us. I basked in the glory of being called a dog whisperer of sorts by friends and acquaintances until I realized I was merely focusing on winning the admiration of animals to avoid adult interaction.

Pets are a convenient safe space. It's just easier to connect with them, which made me feel great, but caused me to miss out on real connections with my fellow humans.

We also expect them to shield us from other emotions in our lives. When a pet dies we avoid processing our grief by getting another one immediately after the loss. When we only have one animal, we get another, projecting our loneliness onto another living creature instead of finding ourselves human friends.

If there is any legitimacy to all those talking animal movies, our pets are probably conversing amongst themselves about their broken owners, and given the opportunity to communicate with us they'd probably say something like:

"All you humans are sitting on your couches in isolation hoping to make a friend, but no one is making the first move. Leave us canines and felines alone, get out there, and make some human friends for yourself!"

If these pets could talk, they sure as hell wouldn't be saying: "Please, I need a friend! Go adopt Frank from the pet store immediately!"

They'd more likely scream: "Stop forcing me to be your friend and let me the fuck out!"

That's an approximate translation, of course. I haven't spoken with many animals lately, so I am speculating based on what I'd be saying if I were in their shoes.

Some owners say their pets have a good life with them. Easy to say that as the master. That hamster you inexplicably trapped in a glass prison its entire life would probably have a different opinion.

Sometimes we mistreat them out of ignorance, as with the poor golden retriever incessantly barking on a nearby condo deck that is barely large enough to fit a lounge chair. I have a sneaking suspicion that panting dogs can't bark as much, so maybe some open space will quiet it down.

Other times we knowingly treat animals poorly.

On the darker side of the emotional spectrum, it appears some of us find enjoyment in exerting power and control over an inferior creature, providing us with a different and more questionable form of emotional support.

Sometimes our treatment is purely a power trip. We tell them what to do, when to do it, how to sit, when to eat, where to pee, where to sleep, and regrettably sometimes when to fight. And if they don't listen we yell, even though we are well aware that they don't speak our language.

Paint any picture you like, but those pets can survive just fine without you.

But can you survive without them?

Think about why you need to *own* another living creature, and how your interactions with them affect you, because that's all it is.

Ownership.

A recurring theme of this book, and a requirement in our *humanity bubble* that we impose upon living beings, inanimate objects, and the earth itself. Think through how we act toward our pets, and note how in conversation we casually mention that we flat out own them.

Not much to refute here.

Head back to all those factory farms and notice how most livestock have an identification number pierced in their ear. That's ownership: a prison sentence within our false reality to make human life easier.

We manipulate the evolution of other species with the norms of our *humanity bubble* because we are convinced that we know better. Dogs are held idle for the length of a human workday, with walks before and after to quickly and intensely exercise muscles meant for constant gentle movement. Cats are forced to relieve themselves in a box, a crude form of the human porcelain throne.

Our inability to steer the evolution of our own species should be a clear sign to leave other species alone, but recall how poorly we read signs like this. In fact, we're probably the only species off-script, which is coincidentally on-brand for humans as we ignore our own very real problems to solve the fabricated issues of other beings that we may or may not have created in our minds.

Devising strategies for making other animals happy is far easier than contemplating our own happiness. "Who rescued who?", we foolishly ask with our bumper stickers. Neither. There is no rescue. That language implies some sort of heroics that just doesn't exist.

We aren't martyrs. We kidnapped these animals from the natural world, trapped them in our *humanity bubble*, manipulated them to suit our needs, and then demanded thanks for such fine treatment.

That dog isn't excited about your presence because you're great.

No single human is that special.

Did you ever have a kid try to butter you up to get what they want? Anyone who has ever heard "Daddy pleeease" from their daughter with the big sad eyes knows how this goes.

That's all these pets are doing, and their end goal is freedom. No animal on this planet needs us. In fact, what they need is for us to leave them be.

They know what to do.

Just last night I watched a hawk preparing a delicious dinner — it was stomping on a dove with its talons.

Dogs bring birds as gifts to the family, which I'll propose they started doing because we bred out of them the understanding that they could actually eat that bird. They forgot what to do so they just carry dead things around now.

I was on a walk one summer morning and I watched a cat cross the street with a small rodent in its mouth.

It was hungry.

It found food.

They don't need your processed cat food. Those cats do need those front claws, though.

They have their own lives to live, and their own purpose to serve in the biosphere. We altered that purpose, and we'll eventually discover the consequences. In the meantime, stop depriving them of a natural existence.

These creatures serve a purpose for us now, but they're slowly being phased out as our primary companions. Replaced but not released, as evidenced by dog walkers these days.

Based on no other supporting information beyond a small sample size I've witnessed in my own neighborhood, I'll extrapolate out and boldly claim that at least half of dog owners aren't even paying attention to their dogs on walks anymore.

Those pet owners found emotional comfort in their newest companion: their cell phone.

Entertainment

We don't seek all our entertainment and companionship from our phones just yet, and consequently there is another subset of animals that play a small role in keeping us amused once our baser needs are met. We're bored now with all this free time our *humanity bubble* provides, and we must be entertained.

So come along with me, and sit next to me by the aquarium for a moment.

Our standard domesticated companions don't quite do it for us, so we occasionally capture the exotic. It is quite nonsensical and seemingly difficult to keep certain species at home, but some people are unphased. Challenge accepted, once more.

That didn't go so well for a local tiger owner, though, so maybe think that one through a bit.

We cage everything from the mundane to the rare. From ostriches, monkeys, bears, and tigers at the zoo — our personal living creature museums — to the mind-boggling assortment of reptiles, amphibians, and fish at aquariums, where at either location we pay another human for the privilege to mindlessly stare at other species.

In other cases, we create rehabilitative sanctuaries. I appreciate the sentiment of saving an injured animal, but a viable alternative is for that wounded animal to be food for another animal, or to just die and give its body back to the earth.

That's an acceptable outcome.

That's how things have always worked on this planet.

Hunting, that task we long ago gave up thanks to grocery stores, has also transitioned from necessity to novelty. We kill animals and then hang the aesthetically appealing once-living trophies on our walls in a more psychologically questionable form of visual pleasure.

Aesthetically appealing to whom, you ask?

Who knows, but just remember, taxidermy doesn't have anything to do with taxicabs, folks.

When we see something rare and exotic, we can't just simply admire its beauty where it exists. It pleases us to have what others don't, so we bring exotic animals from unusual locales to our suburban towns. Their exotic nature and uniqueness somehow makes us feel special because we own a rare creature that we show off to our friends, or we make money by showing it off to an exclusive audience.

We have the technology now to take a high-resolution picture for the socials and move on.

Or just go watch that documentary.

Or get off the couch and go see it yourself.

Or just don't gawk at other creatures and find something better to do with your time. Leave them to prosper right where they are.

It should be clear that these exotic species didn't venture out of the region from which you stole them for a very good reason. Just like those Chihuahuas and Newfoundlands from before, they evolved right there in their *natural* habitat where you originally found them, and right there they should stay.

Just because we humans inexplicably insist on inhabiting every corner of the globe despite being anatomically ill-equipped to survive in such extremes, it doesn't mean other species want the same.

Look no further than the excessive special care, equipment, and *maintenance* certain species require to survive wherever you bring them within our *humanity bubble*.

Just like that stupid lawn you insist on maintaining, if something can't survive naturally, it doesn't belong.

Instead of trying to determine if a tropical reptile could survive in a snowy climate, do the world a favor and just leave the iguana in the fucking rainforest.

We experiment with animals enough as it is.

Experimentation

"Recent pharmaceutical studies have shown the new medication had minimal impact on rats during initial trials, but subsequent trials on rats will be required before continuing on to human testing."

What's the issue with that quote?

Ignore the inaccurate pharma terms in this example as they do not affect my point, and I'm not a pharmaceutical scientist so I don't feel like allocating brain cells to learn them.

It is very likely you see no issue, and that's because we've all normalized experimenting on animals. I recently read a similar line in an actual article, and it took me until after the second mention of rat trials to even react.

We breeze over such talk with indifference and apathy, ignoring the living being that's being discussed and selfishly focusing on the outcome of the next wonder drug for our species.

Clinical trials.

Lab experiments.

Animal testing.

We'll focus on that last one within this section, and start by offering a new definition for *animal testing*:

Forcibly subjecting another living species to unknown, likely damaging, and possibly fatal consequences because humans are too chickenshit to try their outlandish inventions on themselves first.

Humanity bubble growth trumps the lives of other species at this categorical level, and participation in this experimentation of ours is their unwilling contribution to our sustained existence.

Humans that participate in later trials are at least volunteers. Squeezed into desperation by the very system they are signing up to improve, they waive their rights and collect their pithy compensation, but they at least made their own choice, even if it was simply the least bad option.

Other species didn't get that opportunity.

At least I don't think so.

Oh, I really wish all these animals could talk, but I'll once again claim something I didn't first corroborate and say they certainly didn't sign up for this.

Another preposterous sentiment, since rats can't sign anything. Without opposable thumbs, how could they even grip the pen?

With no way to resist our offer to 'help the humans with their science stuff,' these rats are instead treated like a resource to be grown.

A rat died in an experiment? Shame. Thank you for your service, time to grow another one and get back to testing.

All the monkeys that you injected with random diseases got out of the transport vehicle that crashed? Oh well. Shoot 'em and start over.

Investors are becoming impatient, so we must keep going until we get the results we want, and spare no lesser species in the process.

Rats are actually pretty interesting creatures.

I saw one curiously roaming Central Park once, and humans that have kept rats as pets typically marvel at their intelligence.

Hey, at least those *pet* rats made it a few steps up on our hierarchy.

Instead of celebrating their uniqueness, we vilify these rodents as a way to lessen the emotional impact of experimenting on them. The Central Park rat that I saw was up in a sparsely populated wooded area of the park, minding its own business searching for a meal in the brush, but would have caused a panic had it been near a more public location.

We've taken it upon ourselves to decide which animals can serve as guinea pigs for our experimentation, and we've made some interesting choices:

Guinea Pigs. I just used this expression to introduce the list. I have no idea how this phrase joined our lexicon, but your common species name doesn't become a widely used metaphor for experimentation unless your species was at one time used for *something* experimental.

Canaries. The phrase 'canary in a coal mine' isn't some fancy metaphor concocted by Thoreau or Hemingway or Emerson. Apparently, coal miners brought a living breathing bird into the fucking mines to serve as their early warning system.

If there was a presence of poisonous gas at any point, the death of the bird that definitely freely volunteered to descend into the abyss to be a safety alert system for our scared little species would indicate there is still enough time for humans to save themselves.

Blue Crabs. We pull blue crabs out of the water to take their blood, and then toss them back into the water when we are done with them. Not quite full vampire style, since we use tubes and needles instead of our own teeth, and at least we don't kill them.

This route is much better, for someone anyway.

Still not great for the crabs themselves, but kudos to us for only forcibly removing them from their habitat, hooking them up to machines, drawing their blood because it works well in some medical product, and tossing them back in the water.

We feel better about that.

Monkeys. I saw an article about a monkey playing pong on a computer. Why does a monkey need to play pong? What we hope to gain from this particular experiment is a mystery. To see how video games affect the brain? Again, I don't care to research because I don't even like *humans* using a computer, but it's really not complicated.

We use a computer. We become zombies. Test complete.

Once more I'm sure all these animals had better things to do, even if their alternative was to simply exist in the natural world and then die. Even if that monkey merely had to throw poo at another monkey, that would have been better than being forced to use a human imagination machine.

At least poo-slinging is innate behavior for them.

We conclude with a quick nod to the heroic space race that we lost.

No, I'm not Russian.

At least I don't think so.

I am most definitely human, though, and humans lost the space race.

Before we personally braved the vast expanse of outer space, we sent a few other species up first to confirm it would be safe for us.

Thank you for your service, Laika.

To be determined

I'm not being indecisive here.

This title for our last tier of our hierarchy is an apt label for how we view any other species that didn't meet any of the previous criteria.

Pigeons are rats with wings, but these winged rodents escape the same fate as their land-stricken cousins because we have no need to experiment on them — yet.

I always wondered how in the hell we discovered blue crab blood was useful for us, and then I remembered that we meticulously catalog every single species on the planet.

Say it with me everyone: "Kingdom, phylum, class, order..."

We incessantly study them, and occasionally we'll find something useful that results in a species having the distinct honor of climbing the 'usefulness to humans' ladder that we established in that old book of ours with a stroke of a pen or chisel or whatever writing utensil we used back then.

Even though they have no use to us in our *humanity bubble* at the moment, they aren't exactly free either. These stragglers are severely restricted by our presence, since their well-being is another qualitative variable never factored into that mysterious land-value calculation from before. Free to roam but constantly risking death navigating the rapidly vanishing pockets of the natural world between our little *humanity bubble* pixel-cube things.

I'm still not convinced I explained that analogy well.

They remain wholly unaware of the invisible fences formed by our roads, sidewalks, fences, train tracks, and other paths, until they become road-kill.

Why did the opossum cross the road?

It has no fucking clue.

It doesn't even know what a road *is*.

It just walks around like it does everywhere else, but we confound this nocturnal marsupial and all other species with the odd ways in which we alter the surface.

Do I think deer enjoy freezing their asses off up here in the northeast come wintertime?

No.

I'm sure they'd love to migrate; we just clogged any and all means for them to safely move to someplace warmer for the winter. Fortunately for birds, we haven't quite clogged the air space yet, but that time is approaching with our increasingly taller skyscrapers and air taxis.

These animals do serve a purpose, though, despite our flagrant ignorance on the matter. Maybe not directly to us, and not in our *humanity bubble*, but to the greater system *over there* where we are not looking.

They are not directly feeding us or making us feel good or paying us, but they serve as a balance in the system *somewhere*. Otherwise, barring very few exceptions, truly useless species would have naturally disappeared from existence due to that whole evolution thing.

But since they stick around, we take the liberty to provide unsolicited help to our good buddy Darwin by regulating population sizes, for once we categorize stuff we also like to keep track of quantities.

We control species populations

Our categories are all set. It's now time for inventory control.

Type-As rejoice! Order for all!

We *encourage growth* in the population of species that provide value to us:

- Cow meat tastes good? Keep breeding 'em! They'll love their new living arrangements!

- Those salmon are delicious? Start a salmon farm. No need to waste all that time fishing.

- Sheep wool is warm and fuzzy? Expand the flock and start shearing! We lost our fur and don't want to freeze to death.

- This cute little furry canine friend makes me *feel* all warm and fuzzy? Domesticate it, and make sure everyone gets one! We need controllable best friends.

- What a unique animal? Lock it up behind some glass and charge people to see it. Step right up, folks!

- These rodents have similar anatomical systems to us? Grow a human ear on that rat's back. It won't mind!

We *limit* the population of those species that appear to provide no value to us, even though they support us indirectly:

- Ant infestation? Set the traps.

- Spotted lantern fly? Stomp 'em out.

- Too many deer? Let's go hunting.

- Beehive near your deck? Get the insecticide.

- Bear eating your trash? Let's go hunting again.

- Cockroaches? Torch the house and start over.

- Too many scary dogs out there? Put 'em in the pound.

- Animal shelters are suddenly overcrowded with unadoptable animals? Euthanize 'em.

We are the self-proclaimed bean-counters in charge of species population quotas, setting hunting limits with the same level of scrutiny that we set quarterly EPS estimates. We've societally institutionalized these quotas, with at least one federal government having an organizational unit specifically tasked with invasive species control.

The funny thing about our evaluation of invasive species is that we somehow exclude ourselves from that analysis.

Benefits of writing the rules, I suppose.

What's the threshold density for deeming something invasive?

Invasive species are generally considered organisms introduced to a new environment that cause harm to an ecosystem. They reproduce quickly, spread uncontrollably, and outcompete native species for resources.

I guess we successfully excluded ourselves using a technicality involving that whole 'native species' thing, since we conveniently settled down on practically every square meter of the damn planet.

Also well played.

If we could query every other species on this planet, how do you think they'd say things are going? I'll allow you to draw your own parallels there.

Most of these species are just trying to live, but we exterminate them because we either see them as an inconvenience or just find them downright gross. From the vantage point of our *humanity bubble* we increase the good and we limit the bad.

One slight problem.

Our actions conflict with the old-timer, evolution, that has naturally handled this task just fine for the past forever. Equilibrium always returns. One species gets out of line, and the natural world rebalances to maintain order.

Just one more slight problem.

We got out of line while also deciding we are allowed to be out of line, and used our brains to perpetually maintain this misalignment. We have been keeping ourselves in that place ever since, outmaneuvering whatever the planet throws at us to equalize, and normalizing this unbalanced position of ours with the passing of centuries.

We successfully ducked and dived and dodged it all, disrupting the natural balance of the planet by removing all of our natural predators. I would venture to guess that if you are reading this, you have the distinct privilege of saying you have never been hunted by another species.

I have personally never been hunted by another animal.

Have you ever been stalked by another species on your way to the mall? Me neither.

Were you ever stalked by our own species *at any point*? If you've ever dealt with a human predator in any capacity, I apologize on behalf of humanity. I hope you find the closure you deserve, and you can let your story be heard.

We got you.

We stood no chance in unarmed combat against any non-human predator, so we either destroyed them with fun toys we've been able to make — remember those weapons? — or relegated them to the fringes of the natural world outside of our *humanity bubble*.

Those idiots that decided to keep tigers as pets within our fake world weren't as successful.

Congrats on winning a Darwin Award. I'll leave it on your grave.

Murder, we wrote

Murder is terrible.

The word *murder*, as it turns out, is apparently a legal term used to describe the unlawful killing of another *human*, which means all of my notes on how we murder other species suddenly went out the window. At least I didn't have to change that line earlier about animals wanting to murder us.

Resisting the urge to debate what constitutes a *lawful* killing of another human, we will pivot to how we all still *kill* on a mass scale.

We kill out of fear.

We kill for fun.

We kill without reason.

Think of what we do to ants with magnifying glasses, slugs with salt, squirrels with a BB-gun, lightning bugs with a baseball bat, and earthworms with a garden shovel.

All that stupid shit bored kids do.

Since we can't officially call it *murder* based on the definition, we leverage seemingly innocuous words like *exterminate*, a word we frequently use to advertise our lethality toward other species.

A few years ago, a house in my neighborhood proudly displayed an empty bag of insecticide on their lawn, and I can't help but recall the highlighted tagline in the top corner of the bag boasting the number of insect types the product killed. While I appreciate what I can only assume was a warning to alert dog owners that there are chemicals on the ground, if you have to keep animals off it, was it a good idea to apply in the first place?

The weighting we attach to the life of each species drives how we feel about a change in their population numbers.

We, of course, removed ourselves from this scale, since a human life is incomparable to any other living being.

Of course it is. Humans would say that about humans.

Humans, self-imposed judge and jury on who stays and who goes, elevate our own kind above judgement.

Be sterile

We are the first and only species to alter the reproductive organs of any species.

Castrate.

Neuter.

Spay.

Sterilize.

Abstain.

Snip.

-ectomy.

Fun words — and one suffix — that relate to our interference with the reproductive systems of various species. For example, we don't like feral dogs and cats roaming our streets so we 'save them' by 'rescuing them' and then remove their reproductive organs so there can't be more of them.

Noble humans, we are, waging war on the natural process that is reproduction.

We don't go unscathed here.

Medically we find ways to alter the human body's ability to reproduce, and societally we forcibly delay the reproductive process until an arbitrarily decided time that fits our *humanity bubble* best (in case you were wondering how abstain made the list up there).

Then there's that whole surrogacy thing too, another reproductive process humans utilize for themselves and force upon the rest of the natural world.

Despite our best efforts on human population control, I leave you with one more addition to the *limit* list from the start of this chapter:

- Humans overrunning the world? __________________

I'll let you fill in the blank.

We cause extinction

How many species have gone extinct on our watch?

I have no idea, but given that we maintain an endangered species list, the answer has to be greater than zero.

I know us — we would never proactively start a list like that.

Some species just can't hang with our global redecorating. We actually *"Murica'ed"* so hard over here that we almost killed off our quintessential symbol of freedom.

DDT for all, and for all a mosquito-free night. Also, no more bald eagles. Whoops!

At least we got our act together and they are on the rebound.

Yay us!

Hero syndrome once more, as humans valiantly save other species from the disastrous fate originally inflicted on them by their saviors.

Similarly, we perceive ourselves winning the Darwin games thanks to our advancement, but we unfortunately misunderstand the rules. We cluelessly pursue superiority in a game that rewards balance.

We're celebrating a high score of 150 without realizing we're inexplicably on a damn golf course again, and should have as low a score as possible.

I am getting ahead of myself slightly, but based on this book title I'm clearly betting on a new claim to fame for our species: causing *our own* extinction.

Not exactly something I can write down after the fact, so you [maybe] heard it here first!

A seemingly outlandish claim until you recall that nuclear weapons count from earlier.

Our hunt for all things exotic

Back to all those exotic earth-neighbors of ours and some fun terminology: poaching.

I can poach an egg, but if I'm a poacher, I'm not an egg chef.

I can also poach top talent from the competition, but if I'm a poacher, I'm not a highly-skilled recruiter either.

If I'm a poacher, I'm a killer of an exotic animal for fun or profit.

Whether the end goal is to harvest all or part of their bodies, we seem to like hunting them in particular, and on our quest to acquire what our human species has inexplicably deemed desirable, we drive them to the point of extinction.

Elephant tusks and rhino horns, weird shit like that.

Why?

I have no clue.

Growing up, I vaguely recall my home having some sort of elephant tusk thingy on our wall for some reason, and I was afraid to ask my father about it. His answer to my question about our family origins was to tell me we're English because our name appears on the cover of an English dictionary, so I feared the preposterous answer he would give me for why we prominently displayed that trophy in our den.

While I cannot explain any of these hunting decisions, I actually encourage you to go for it. Keep killing for sport!

Just do it with your bare hands.

No pistols or rifles.

No spears or bows.

No nets or snares.

Go punch a lion in the fucking face and let me know how that goes for you.

In some cases, we'll shamelessly strip these animals of their defense mechanisms and pat ourselves on the back because we were humane and didn't kill the animal, as if that creature is now somehow better off thanks to our interference.

That animal simply forgot about the endowed but also self-granted right of humans to help themselves to the bodies of inferior species, rendering them defenseless, docile, and helpless.

Returning from the savannah, consider a few examples closer to home, like how we de-claw cats, trim the beaks and wings of birds, and castrate oxen. We constantly remove natural parts of animals and make them defenseless.

Story of our lives.

Imagine the furor humans would raise if we forcefully removed their unalienable right to self-defense.

Our Relationship Amongst Ourselves

We suck at doing nothing

Go outside and sit still on the ground for five minutes.

No phone.

No external stimuli.

Nothing.

Just close your eyes and remain still on the ground for five minutes.

Sounds easy, right? Too much for you? Try one minute if that seems easier. Can't tolerate sitting on the ground outside? Try it on the floor inside first.

This task is not easy because as a species we have lost the ability to remain mentally and physically still.

If you are like me, all sorts of randomness flashes through your brain in those first few seconds of idleness. Your entire to-do list probably rattles through your brain in completely random order, and your brain demands that *now* is the time to reorder it.

Perhaps your brain throws in a few random memories and thoughts that serve no purpose other than to keep the wheels turning up there.

Thoughts like:

- What ever happened to that middle school girlfriend of mine? I hope she's doing well, and that she found someone nice to marry. Wait a minute, I didn't even start dating until high school.

- What should I make for dinner tonight? Tacos sound good, but do I have meat defrosted? Are those avocados ripe yet? Wait, we can't have tacos tonight. It's not Tuesday!

- Did the local sports team play last night? I hope they won the match-game-event-series-showdown. Hooray for sports!

- Who really did fire the opening shot in that first movie oddly labeled as the fourth episode chronicling wars happening in the stars?

- And my personal favorite: did I leave the stove on? I didn't even use it today, yet I still somehow may have left it on. I should go check just in case.

Most humans can barely achieve five seconds of doing nothing, unlike that lazy feline that inspired this book.

Doing is good, though, right?

What do other species do?

Well, everybody else conserves their energy until it is absolutely necessary to exert it, and it's almost always spent seeking out a meal. Solid logic right there, since they typically don't know when their next meal is coming.

They also partake in some additional strenuous and explosive physical activity to keep their species going, but we can skip that for now.

During a group tour of the outback many moons ago, our guide, who I'll just call Bob, explained how crocodiles — an ancient species crushing it in the longevity game — could survive for a few weeks on the whole chicken he was feeding them. That croc, an animal that could effortlessly dismember even the strongest of humans, can survive on so little because it exerts so little.

It predominantly chills out on a riverbank catching some rays while it scans its territory for a meal, a few sexy croc-mates, or invaders. Yes, the tiny croc brain certainly reduces the energy burn rate too, but that small brain is developed enough to ascertain better than we can that it makes more sense to remain idle on the riverbank conserving energy instead of swimming laps as a great way to stay in shape.

Sure, it could do that, but why waste the energy?

Not us, though.

Constant motion and productivity are requirements to keep our *humanity bubble* humming along, while other species merely look on in amazement at our daily energy waste.

We turn and burn through resources at a rate unseen by any species on this planet ever. Eight-plus billion mini-powerplants running frantically across the surface of the earth, pointlessly burning the candle at 16 ends, desperately scouring the earth and beyond for new fuel sources to maintain our feverish pace.

Our obsessive obligation to be on the move, to incessantly think, and to constantly keep our idleness at bay all burn energy.

Moving my damn pinky, as basic as it seems, expends *some* energy.

That stillness exercise we all failed at the beginning of this chapter burned energy too, because our minds insisted on constant thought. Not much, but it was an energy expenditure nonetheless. Optional usage that compounded atop our basic metabolic rate, that bare minimum benchmark of energy consumption needed to keep us alive. All energy burn above that rate is a choice.

My buddy Bob had another keen observation on that wild tour down under in the outback.

He commented on how we fuel up our bodies for the sole purpose of running a race, we run the race, then we refuel our bodies after the race to replace the energy we just burned.

Energy expended in a matter of hours to accomplish a task that brought everyone to an arbitrary end point that may have also been the starting point. An individual energy burn over a few hours that could have powered a human at normal levels for a few days.

The term *marathon* derives from a specific transit in Greek times, but leave it to modern day humans to make light of the delivery of a serious message by unnecessarily burning excessive energy running that same distance just to say we could, and instead of arriving at a new destination with a purpose, we show up at the finish line, call it a day, and head back home.

We aim for efficiency in every single one of our engineered energy-consuming systems, while completely ignoring any sort of natural energy efficiency for our own bodies.

We liberally choose this life since our fuel is readily available.

We have reserves stored in our pantries and our refrigerators at home, with additional reserves at the grocery store and a backup to that backup at distribution warehouses. If the food supply runs out, a good percentage of us also have a third-tier backup in the form of excess energy stored in our bodies.

Even the few extra kilos I carry around, trivial as they may be, count as a reserve of sorts. Don't worry, I'll fit back into all those suits in my closet any day now.

We may have a multi-century track record of the shelf being our primary source of sustenance, but expand your timeline to say — I don't know — maybe the full range of humanity, and our amazing track record becomes a rounding error relative to our old ways.

We laud our achievement in not having to worry about where our next meal is coming from, but are we truly better off because of it?

One would assume we would eventually challenge this mentality, since we appear somewhat concerned about how to feed our population in the next 30 years.

As the rest of the species world remains idle and conserves energy, we churn through our food sources at an alarming rate, convinced we'll re-actively save ourselves with a miraculous engineering solution after the pantry runs empty.

We eat more than our bodies need, and do more in a given day than is necessary, burning precious energy in the process.

Now I would love to proclaim that this chapter is an advocacy campaign for perpetual laziness. I am on a sabbatical of sorts as I type these words, so I assure you I would love nothing more than to *not* return to the corporate grind.

I'm doing everything in my power *not* to, but I've worked more on this break than I did while employed, putting in seven days a week on this little writing project for months. Someday I'll cease my war on boredom and instead set my sights on waging a new war against productivity.

We should all do the same.

There is nothing wrong with being bored.

It is okay to do nothing.

Boredom isn't a flaw or a disease; it is a sign that you do not need to be entertained.

It is a sign of true freedom.

We refuse to hibernate

Winters are ROUGH in the higher latitudes, and rising before the sun becomes a struggle during those short, cold days.

Wouldn't it be great to simply remain idle until spring?

A lofty goal, but if we can barely sit still for five minutes, there is no way in hell we could ever hibernate for a few months.

Our bodies instinctively know resting is the right move. Our inner voice begs us to remain in bed, but the *humanity bubble* sends its siren's song to lure us from our slumber, and we fully commit to our school, work, and appointment obligations regardless of external environmental conditions. We consciously override our body's primal alarms and soldier on with our premature arisal.

Arisal. Not arousal.

We obediently adhere to the societal systems that demand we continuously operate around the clock, and around the calendar.

Meanwhile, every other species on the planet knows when to reduce bodily energy use and settle in for the winter. Most of our fellow mammals — bears, squirrels, chipmunks, rabbits — put up the "Will return in a few months" sign and disappear until the weather and food prospects improve.

Insects have it a little worse off, as they simply die off and their offspring rise again in the spring to carry the flag of their respective species.

Others remain visible but subdued, as they are well aware food is sparse during these times. They read the seasons and adjust their energy output accordingly. They may actually wish to migrate, but recall that we've made transit so dangerous that the threat of freezing to death is the better option compared to becoming roadkill.

All creatures, including humans, were forever faced with choosing dormancy or death, but here come humans with a better way: the global supply chain.

We're the only species exerting energy when our means of replenishing that energy remain sparse. We carry on in the name of productivity and continuous improvement thanks to our reliance on shipping from *over there*, and any mention of human hibernation would surely elicit the following general responses:

- How will I pay for housing?

- What will I do during all that time, just sit there?

- I'll be bored. My brain could never stay idle that long.

- I have to eat eventually; how will I afford food?

- I'll lose my job.

- I need to see friends.

- I could never sleep that long.

- My competitors will outpace me if I rest that long.

- My business will close.

And then my personal favorite, since the economy knows no seasons:

- *If I rest, I'm not making money.*

So human hibernation is out of the question.

You know it.

I know it.

It's downright impractical and these concerns are all very reasonable. As much as I'd love to sleep for months, I'd go stir crazy if I didn't move for that long.

The mass paranoia that would ensue is also obvious, and I'd bet the mere thought of shutting down for three months immediately sent you spiraling. You'd have that sneaking suspicion that you should be doing something.

That societal guilt of idleness.

We absolutely refuse to rest because resting is frowned upon in our *humanity bubble*, and we see it as lazy and unproductive, regardless of the very clear signs that we shouldn't expend energy.

But asking why we don't hibernate is the wrong question.

We should collectively be asking why we have accepted a system that prevents us from slowing down during the months when our essentials are sparse.

Every other species follows their primal instincts here, pulling back based on their innate sense that the earth is not producing. It's simple and straightforward.

They.

Pull.

Back.

Meanwhile we push on in the other direction, demanding and drawing from the earth to fuel ourselves everywhere, all the time.

Can't wake up in the morning? Here's an alarm clock and some coffee. Get moving.

Can't see in the dark? Here's a flashlight, you'll be fine. We are an apex predator now, nothing out there will get you.

Food doesn't grow in the extreme latitudes during winter? No problem. Grow it *over there* and ship it in.

There isn't a single deer in Slovakia eating leaves and flowers imported from Uruguay, and you don't see rabbits in Ireland eating clover import-ed from Morocco.

Those behaviors sound comical when we project them onto an animal, but when we trace it back to humans it's suddenly normal.

We remain opportunistic.

We see a pullback by others as the time to strike. Never mind the fact that others are pulling back for sensible reasons.

Here comes the rain

A rainy day is a beautiful opportunity to cozy up on the couch and enjoy nature at work. The experience is therapeutic, yet humans view rain as a considerable inconvenience. While those little cubes that form our humanity bubble are in our minds impenetrable, the elements still find their way through to dampen our day.

How do you feel when it rains?

Do you refuse to get out of bed?

Do you lament having to go outside in wet conditions?

Our bodies naturally avoid the rain, but we go out in the downpour anyway because our societal systems necessitate it. Just look at the army of umbrellas bopping along the streets of any major city on a rainy day.

We're the only species that's unwise enough to slog out into the rain to get to a desk and sit in a chair that destroys our posture and stare at a screen that deteriorates our eyesight.

Other species rest when it rains, venturing out only to find something to eat, or maybe take a shower. Once they've fulfilled their needs, they return to their cover and wait out the weather.

Not us.

We have those umbrellas and carports and valets and raincoats and rain boots and garages.

Snowy day? We have shovels and rock salt and brine and scrapers and crazy 18-wheeler-sized contraptions that can launch snow 50 meters away.

Why would we possibly need to stay inside when all our inventions help clear the way to work?

I would never expect my boss to accept my staying home because of an ongoing deluge. I get it. Our *humanity bubble* obligates us to show up on rainy days, end of story.

So, we do.

And we always will.

That feeling that tells you to stay put?

That would be our primal instincts that we keep ignoring, and we are no doubt the only ones overriding those signals.

Our invasion of darkness

Human beings have no business being out at night. Our bodies aren't built for nocturnal operations.

We can't see a damn thing out there, and we are scared shitless by a rustling in the leaves. The other night a moth the size of my hand flew at me and I almost ran right through my unopened door trying to get back inside, frantically fleeing that beastly moth that was merely thinking, "Oooo, look at that pretty bright light."

Thankfully we've eliminated all of our natural predators, but quite frankly we are helpless out there when the sun goes down.

We've created neat gadgets like flashlights, headlights, night vision goggles, and flares — all flashy tech that we can take on the move — but who wants to constantly carry around all that gear?

Light bulb! Let's just perpetually light up the darkness with more permanent innovations, allowing us to function at all hours without the burden of bringing our own portable light sources.

Most species that are aware of their inability to function at night just don't go out at night. Solid logic once more for all those intellectually inferior species.

They stay hidden until the light returns, sticking with the simple solution that allows them to safely navigate the world.

Do we follow suit?

Of course not. Onward with this war on darkness and our relentless pursuit of technological advancement sustaining our campaign.

Revisiting our lighting example, our energy-efficient lighting options allow us to light up the entire world, and we find ways to illuminate objects that were previously unlit.

We illuminate indoor building spaces around the clock for the security cameras keeping watch over our valuables.

The façades of commercial and residential buildings are covered in around-the-clock lighting too. It looks nice, though, and nobody can sneak up when we cast a perpetual light on the perimeter.

The shade, the shadows, the darkness. We erase it all thanks to advancements in lighting technology.

From threats, both human and not.

But the world needs darkness, in the same way that the earth mysteriously needs that radiant energy now being hijacked by those solar panels we install everywhere.

Again, I couldn't tell you *why* we need it, but I can easily surmise that demanding perpetual and omnipresent light on a planet that maintained a stable, natural cycle of light and dark for fucking eons might disrupt a few things.

Something has changed: we just can't see it yet.

Better whip out a flashlight to take a better look.

Ecological processes are occurring at night that support our ability to walk the earth during the day, and our refusal to believe that fact doesn't change reality. The world is at work from dusk till dawn, and while most of us may be sleeping and idle at those hours, we are a paranoid lot so we ignorantly and destructively charge forward to light up the world at all times.

Nothing will stand in our way.

Just ask the sperm whale population that nearly went extinct stingily withholding from us the oil from their bodies that we 'needed' in order to keep our lamps alight in the 19th century.

Curing leisurephobia

We successfully avoided leisure and secured our ability to function around the clock across the globe.

We continue our advance, because that's what we do.

If we slow down in the winter, if we stand idle, the vaguely defined, passionately vilified, and conveniently unidentifiable enemy will move under the cover of darkness and get us.

If we rest in the rain, our adversaries will be at our doorstep as the rain subsides and the clouds part.

If we sleep at night, we will awaken to being behind in the morning.

This unbridled and unhealthy paranoia is a gravely misplaced internal concern that life is fucked if we rest, causing us to pursue constant productivity to keep our *humanity bubble* running, so we diligently watch the clock waiting for the perfect opportunity to strike.

We insist on knowing the time

Time was forever measured by day and night.

Now we have the zeptosecond.

We can't necessarily take credit for creating time as a general concept. Try as we may to claim that one, we'll leave that distinguished honor to Father Time.

We are, however, responsible for quantifying it, tracking it, breaking it down into infinitesimally smaller increments, and monetizing it.

Time. A uniquely human obsession. Our greatest downfall, and our new master.

We could never realistically remove it from our lives right now. We are stuck for the moment, and the world as we know it would fall apart If we tried to immediately break free. We would be late to work, our kids would miss practice, and we would show up to the airport on the wrong day.

Meanwhile, no other species knows what time it is.

No other species knows what time *is*.

In line with the rest of the natural world, every other species acknowledges nothing more granular than daylight and darkness.

No other species on this planet wears a watch, owns a clock, or sets an alarm. They generally sleep in darkness and arise with the sun, with the reverse holding true for our nocturnal friends who follow a similar but flip-flopped binary schedule.

They have no interest in anything more specific. They just don't care, unless we make them care, like those crated dogs anxiously awaiting the end of the workday so they can relieve themselves.

Having somewhere to be is a purely human state of being, so I envy those that avoid tracking time so closely.

Lucky bastards.

Our obsession with continuous improvement has caused us to take that once universally accepted, binary time measurement system — day and night — and dissect it down further and further into ever smaller divisions.

Slicing and Dicing the clock

For those of you out there that are still wondering, a zeptosecond is 0.000000000000000000001 seconds.

I'll spare you the eye strain: there are 20 zeros after the decimal point.

It's a unit of measure we devised to quantify the time it takes a light particle to cross a hydrogen molecule. It apparently takes 247 zeptoseconds, by the way, for all you aspiring trivia gameshow contestants out there.

Will humans leverage this information in the name of growth and advancement? Of course. I have no doubt that very smart people are doing something with this information right now.

Will the resulting innovations prove useful? Maybe, but only in our *humanity bubble*.

Does the average individual need this information? Nope.

Did the natural world function just fine without us measuring a zeptosecond? You bet it did.

We constantly fragment time. We account for every second of our days in much the same way we quantify and categorize other things:

- All land is divided up down to the very last meter.

- Every cubic centimeter of our homes contains stuff.

- Every resource on the planet is used to maximum efficiency.

- Nearly every animal on the planet has been identified, catalogued, and inventoried.

The hands of the clock — yes, those two pointers on an analog clock are called hands — dictate our lives as we aim to productively allocate every last second in our day.

Bus stop at 0800, meetings at 0900, 1000, 1100, and 1200. Lunch at 1300. Client meetings in the afternoon from 1400-1600, and hopefully someone got to the bus stop for afternoon pickup. Sports activities at 1700. Dinner at 1930, with maybe a bit of TV afterwards. Sleep by 2100. Repeat.

A standard day in the US of A, with the exception of that annoying [to some] 24-hour time system. Society has blessed us with this construct, and we feel unproductive if we don't obey the rules.

We are incapable of handling unstructured time. Play dates with friends are scheduled weeks in advance like medical appointments. The entire calendar is filled with pre-planned activities, leaving no room for deviation or any unstructured activities. We cannot even go on a vacation anymore without structure. Staff hand us an itinerary, or the moment our trip starts we download an app that tells us where to be at each hour.

Nature is chaos, but chaos creates panic in our *humanity bubble.* We shall have order, and maintaining that order — or returning to order from a state of disarray — generates a sense of satisfaction in us.

A sense of achievement.

A sense of productivity.

A *false* sense of calm.

Our obsession with time drives us to do crazy things:

- Anxiety induced by the fact that we won't arrive at a location at a specific time.

- Fear of losing something substantial if we don't submit deliverables by a certain date.

- Panic from realizing we missed a payment and will be charged heavily for the error.

- Anger arising when something doesn't happen on time.

- Frustration from yelling at kids that are not ready to leave the house on time ("If I had a nickel...").

Even as I freely write some of these drafts, I feel like I should be doing something more productive with my time, because according to our society writing is not truly productive.

It's all a choice. A choice we collectively make as we hang out at practice every Saturday afternoon, standing in an open field sweating or freezing for the sake of sports and our kids.

Our bodies know it is wrong.

We do it anyway.

Trusting our internal clocks

When did you last make it an entire day without checking the time?

I can't answer that for myself, but you know who could if we had the right translator? These cats right next to me.

Our minds are time-obsessed, but our bodies dismiss the norms we built in our crazy world. Get sick enough and your body takes control without concern for the time of day, or what you owe your boss.

Instinct trumps intellect here, and thankfully our *humanity bubble* hasn't had enough time to evolutionarily infect our immune system with new operating instructions.

Your body needs what it needs, when it needs it, regardless of any human-defined, time-sensitive requirements.

We see this in the outright rejection of time when our bodies flip into survival mode, like during a recent ailment of mine where I was going to bed at 1900, waking up at 0330, taking a quick shower, and then eating around 0400.

In an affront to the standard human-defined meals we'll review shortly, I found myself standing in front of the fridge randomly eating a carrot right out of the bag, ripping off a handful of kale from the stalk, and chowing down on a few mini bell peppers.

Your body intrinsically knows what it needs, and it doesn't give a damn what you *think* you need.

Living without the burden of time

There is no more freeing state than losing track of time during the course of a day.

Electronic devices away, no clock in sight.

This is no small feat.

I personally have over a dozen devices in my house that display the time, all of which somehow stubbornly refuse to show the *exact* same time.

During a recent writing session, I snapped out of my flow-state to realize I had no idea what time it was. No other agenda, nowhere to be, and no child activities requiring my chauffeur services.

It was wonderful.

Blissful.

Serene.

Admittedly, a few mojitos and enchiladas were involved that day.

On another occasion I legitimately couldn't recall what day it was. Old age isn't setting in — yet. I was just a month or two into my time off, and the days started blending together since I had no useless deadlines or obligations demanding my attention.

We are obsessed with knowing the time and miss out on the freedom that comes with ignoring it. That cathartic feeling of liberating our minds from the burden of time, forgetting it exists in any measurable form, and dismissing the unsubstantiated requirement to constantly monitor this arbitrary concept that we alone acknowledge as real.

We fail to simply be present and break free from the chains of time.

What slaves we have become to this heavily quantified time system, and we obediently attack anyone who isn't rising with the alarm to seize the day and be productive.

Carpe Diem everyone. YOLO for you young folk.

The cats have it right with the lounging life, but we convinced ourselves that we, as the dominant ones, have a better way. We can accomplish amazing feats with our complex brains, but with that ability comes a mandate for constant productivity and efficiency.

We sheepishly obey the clocks around us, selling off our time to the highest bidder in exchange for a number shown to us on an imaginary box that indicates we have enough credits to buy all these wants disguised as needs. We obediently behave this way for the first 60 years of life until we finally earn the right to rest that we've been inexplicably denied all our lives.

So, as we putz away the zeptoseconds managing 14 different digital calendars, seven alarms, and myriad deadlines, the rest of the planet continues to operate with a simpler time structure. We fail to comprehend that decades matter more while stubbornly insisting that every second counts.

We require perpetual growth

We cannot stay still.

We cannot slow down.

We cannot hibernate.

We cannot take our eyes off the clock.

We cannot waste a minute resting.

We cannot leave land in an undeveloped state.

The physical items in our *humanity bubble* may be subject to decay, but our constant growth mindset is immune to such decomposition.

Continuous improvement is ubiquitous in our imaginary world, but how can a planet of fixed physical volume and a set resource inventory possibly support perpetual human growth?

Spare me any talk of acquiring more resources through all that M^2 bull-shit — Move to Mars, Mine the Moon. We already walked through what Jevon had to offer on efficient and responsible resource usage, so you are fooling yourself if you think we would actually curtail our consumption once we've Swiss-cheesed the lunar surface.

If we're irresponsible enough with the resources on this planet to even *consider* space mining, we won't use those minerals well either.

A lack of available resources isn't the issue here.

And yet we maintain steady, consistent growth. Why?

No one can clearly articulate its necessity, aside from an army of uptight experts stressing its importance using circular arguments, and insisting that any rejection of this premise will cause the whole economic system to crash.

Sacrosanct principles haunt us once more.

We need growth to keep our *humanity bubble* humming along, and we *want* the accompanying adrenaline rush that comes with pushing the limits, which is fine until a few insufferable, ego-driven bipeds get carried away racking up all-time high scores in the net worth game.

Our inexplicable, insatiable desire for growth drives our competitiveness and negatively influences our decisions as we push further from our natural state of being, and that lurking paranoia of ours periodically resurfaces to falsely remind us that complacency invites defeat.

This behavior is unnatural.

It is unhealthy.

It's not what's really happening.

Humans, resigned to the fate of Sisyphus, pushing that boulder up an endless hill for eternity, which we accept since we're here to play that infamous *infinite* game — playing without any specific outcome in mind — that ignores the very *finite* constraints of this world. We never truly make any progress as we continue to burn up real resources on what we thought was an imaginary hill.

By setting our annual goals as relative measures — 5% annual growth, or 2% annual inflation, sophisticated figures like that — we all but guarantee an unsustainable trajectory of attempting to grow forever, with no end in sight.

Weird growth habits

What would happen if we just stopped growing for a year?

The economy would probably grind to a halt, chaos would ensue, my retirement accounts would crash at the worst possible time, and economists would be screaming in sheer panic.

Our ways demand that we constantly generate new leads, increase cash flow, make new deals, renegotiate old deals to achieve better terms, and earn more money than last year. We strive for more followers, likes, and clicks, all of which somehow generate more money to buy way more than just our essentials.

We think we *need to* but we merely *want to*, for whatever personal reasons we've locked in on, and where does that lead us?

Indirect price increases and shrinking amenities

Rewards programs periodically and incrementally chip away at benefits, disguising true consumer value with obscure point systems and clandestinely devaluing each point we earn over time.

The subtly shrinking chip bags seem just slightly less full, effectively increasing the unit cost.

Restaurants recently started passing credit card fees on to customers.

Comfortable cabanas at water parks were once gratis and are now for rent as a separate charge.

I have a hard time finding a gas station with free compressed air to fill my tires.

It's why those airplane seats we brought up earlier keep getting smaller, and also why airplane manufacturers are considering double-decker seating on planes to make room for more lucrative seating options up front. Don't think it can happen? Coach class airline seats were basically the size of business class seats in the 50's.

Loss of ownership

Outright ownership is a thing of the past. I still have my CDs and DVDs in the basement from decades ago, but the world around us is evolving toward subscription models. CD players are slowly phasing out of stores and automobiles.

On at least two occasions I've seen songs I enjoy disappear from the music streaming service I use.

They were there. Then suddenly they weren't.

Streaming services remove or alter originally innocuous but suddenly controversial TV episodes from their platforms.

You want something? We'll keep it safe for you in the cloud and you can pay us to access it. Will it be there tomorrow? Will we alter it in the background between your access dates?

Who knows?

Futile feature creep

Why does my text message background need to show me an animated short when someone writes "lol" or "congratulations"? I can envision a person laughing out loud without the damn wacky waving inflatable tube man in the background. I recently wrote someone a quick "Happy Halloween" text and my phone assaulted me with a digital barrage of bats, vampires, and pumpkins. My screen went white and reindeer flew across my screen as I said "Merry Christmas" to friends.

Also, I can't help but wonder how the weird cell phone contraption was actively aware that I wrote "Halloween" and not "Christmas" in my message, and was able to launch the proper animation.

Quality loss

We optimize the shit out of everything now, and nothing lasts these days because we've sacrificed longevity for manufacturing efficiency. Using 15% less material because an equation said we could is great for the bottom line, but that extra material historically offset all those unknown unknowns that surfaced when nature throws our meticulous plans in the trash.

We buy companies for their 100-year history of manufacturing high quality products, continue highlighting the old company's quality track record and century-old establishment date on our new packaging, then fail to mention the significant quality degradation we caused by implementing cost-cutting measures to justify the acquisition.

I'll spare the excess examples here and close this one with the standard old-guy "they don't make 'em like they used to" proclamation.

Perpetual expansion

Our constant need for growth, expansion, and change is what drives every other food company to come up with increasingly more ridiculous concoctions each year. It's why a basic dessert like cookies suddenly has enough variety to occupy an entire grocery store aisle.

Look at house sizes of a century ago versus today. Look at the size of an RV today compared to house sizes a century ago. Look at the number of houses per person these days.

Holiday inflatable decorations on front lawns that were once knee-high are now roof-high.

I can now play video games through my music streaming app.

My language app teaches math and chess.

Did you know credit agencies have rewards programs now? When we do such a good job spending money we don't have, we are now rewarded with the opportunity to spend even more through special offers prominently displayed on their websites while the core functions we truly need remain buried.

I can now own one ten-thousandth of a share of stock that can be valued in ten-thousandths of a penny.

I can even own a fractional share of a racehorse.

A 90-minute movie could typically tell a full story and our minds could fill in any plot holes. Individual movies now run two-plus hours, and multiple prequels and sequels take our imaginations out of the equation while also forming a steady project pipeline for studios.

The phrase 'Christmas in July' no longer implies what it used to because stores are now prepping for Christmas ads in summer.

Companies that previously specialized in one product or industry are now conglomerates that own everything from weapons to insurance to ball bearings to cookware to banks to NFTs to food products to satellites to furniture.

It's why a carmaker's model lineup grows over the years. The compact sedan suddenly becomes the mid-sized sedan, with a new smaller model filling the compact segment, and for some reason that new vehicle jumps on the 'light up everything' bandwagon and includes a multi-colored illuminated grill emblem and all sorts of accent lighting in the cabin.

The medium-sized truck is now suddenly the size of the full-size truck from five years ago, and the new full-size model is a fucking boat. Seriously, Mr. 'Average Height' over here can barely see into the truck cabin from a crosswalk, but the advent of sensors and cameras and radar and lidar absolve drivers of the responsibility to keep watch. No need to look because if someone or something is there the vehicle will send the driver a notification.

This fancy technology creates a clear path toward autonomous vehicles that will allow us to gain back precious time for ourselves during our commute, but what if we just spent less time in the car?

Our frame of reference has become distorted, and our decisions support constant growth of our *humanity bubble*.

But at least we can have dinner underwater now, or sleep in an ice palace.

Hallelujah.

From chucking spears to throwing spirals

The western world is obsessed with sports. Back in my day...

That's right, *clichés for days* in this book — and they'll keep coming.

Back in my day, I went to practice a few days a week, played games on the weekends, finished the season, and went on with my life.

My basketball coach once asked how I spent my time each summer in an attempt to steer me toward a basketball camp. I still wonder to this day if he thought I had potential, or similar to the remedial intent of summer school, he felt I needed a little extra help on the court.

We'll never know.

I declined and explained that summer was my skateboarding time. Basketball was just something I played recreationally to stay active, and didn't feel the need to play in the off-season.

And let's be real, as athletically inclined as I felt I was back then, I was rocking that average height that prevents me from seeing over truck hoods, along with an average overall build while living in a small community. A standout in my small suburban hometown, I would barely register on a scouting report the moment I stepped beyond city limits.

If only I had practiced more. That's the attitude of today's youth, pretty much the moment they can walk.

Practice consumes today's athletes most nights during the week for hours at a time, and then they have camps in between the seasons and additional training on days where there is no formal practice.

If it's too cold to practice, we build all these indoor practice facilities and field houses to continue our training year-round, once more enclosing a small portion of the natural world to get a few extra reps in when the weather is *le bad*.

Sports were once just hobbies that regular people partook in to exercise and demonstrate the athletic abilities they honed outside of their normal life, but now we breed athletes from the ground up. They are mere machines, custom-designed and crafted for performance and financial engineering.

That's a fancy way of saying they generate money. Think of what the team owners must be earning if they can afford to pay athletes what they pay them.

Consequently, each athlete exists to compete in their single sport. Multi-sport, Jack-of-all-trades athletes are gone, because if you don't specialize you'll fall behind. If you didn't start playing the moment you launched out of your mother, you're already behind.

Sports are now an arduous job, requiring exponentially more time beyond the standard nine-to-five, along with other dietary and behavioral commitments that I imagine render life just a bit unenjoyable. Your purpose is sport, and if you break, doctors deploy their medical innovations to return you to service.

We've turned what was once a leisurely activity into a job, in the name of optimization, to be the best we can at something.

Why?

We are hell-bent on being the best, of course. The human condition of one-upmanship and a need to perpetually grow both run rampant throughout our lives as we push the limits of what's possible, break the records set before us, and honor the thrones upon which the legends of our respective sports currently sit.

Let's be honest, if the greats were here today they'd be confused. Mickey Mantle would rise out of his coffin and wonder why the hell he's being asked to cut into his drinking time.

Our constant growth fixation has invaded our leisure, sucking the enjoyment out of life and misdirecting our attention toward pursuits that support our *humanity bubble* but serve no purpose out in the natural world, because while athletes may be fit, that type of fitness is a poor substitute for the primal physical activity we truly need.

So long Mom and Pop

During a trip to the local hardware store back in my late teens, I realized I forgot my wallet as I approached the register to buy a small lawnmower part.

That would be my physical wallet, by the way. The technology for paying with your phone or your palm or your retinas was at least a decade away at the time, and I had no first-born to offer up as an alternative form of payment.

I left the part on the counter and told the cashier I would return, but the store owner was near the register and overheard our conversation.

Owner: "Go ahead, just take the part."

Me: "What's that now?"

Owner: "Take the part. What's the worst that could happen? You don't come back and I'm out $7? I can take that hit. I'm not going to come hunt you down over $7."

I immediately returned with the money, and during the ride I attempted to process what the hell just happened.

Go into a store today and tell the cashier that you forgot your method of payment and see if you are given the same opportunity to leave with the item.

N-.

F------.

W--.

Hell, go into a large store today and ask for help, and the store worker is likely checking for the item on a handheld device, then giving you a curt answer and going back to what they were doing, annoyed that you didn't simply go on your own phone and search the inventory yourself through their app.

When competition eliminates small, local, multi-generational shops — those 'mom and pop' stores that have been open for half a century or more — we lose more than a place to buy things.

We lose our sense of community. Our real-life social interactions. Our ability to trust each other. To simply converse with each other.

To give each other a fucking break once in a while.

We all need one from time to time.

We lost those stores because they didn't *want* to compete financially. Their purpose wasn't to drive the competition to bankruptcy. Their purpose wasn't to optimize. I'm not a business major, but I will safely assume there's a part of the boutique in-store experience that doesn't get factored into the purely financial equation used to value a business. These shops merely enjoyed providing something to their community, so they provided it.

No ulterior motive.

No expansion strategies to penetrate new markets.

No profit margin growth requirements.

No arbitrarily derived quarterly EPS estimates to meet.

It only takes one, though.

One obsessed and likely paranoid individual to trigger the chain reaction and ruin it for the rest of us, emboldening others to unleash their competitive nature. This pissing contest of ours culminates in a select few pushing way out of balance and consolidating the market, which eventually instills in those few successful consolidators at the top of the mountain a preordained right to do some seriously stupid shit with their unfathomably large account balances.

Say it with me one last time — "You do you!"

We need community.

I still haven't become a psychologist in the 150 or so pages since first attempting to psychoanalyze something, but I don't need a piece of paper hanging on my wall to know that going to the store where you are known by name creates a positive psychological experience.

You leave with more than the product or service you sought upon entering, but we're too busy for that now, especially when everything we need is dropped off right to our front door by a different person for each delivery because we can order through our phones now.

Convenience?

Or a way by which we are unknowingly and intentionally being disconnected from the human interactions that keep us grounded?

I'll never know for sure, but I do know that as a mere occasional coffee drinker I frequent a certain coffee shop that's off my normal route because of the amazing positive atmosphere I experience there.

And yes, for those still wondering about that hardware store from before, it closed down a few years ago.

Invest in farmland

Hey, how about we turn the land that was originally meant to feed us into an investment vehicle to generate money for financial portfolios?

What could possibly go wrong?

Farms are meant to feed us and not our bank accounts, but now they must entertain us and enrich us. Nearly every farm around me that hasn't been lured by the lucrative paycheck associated with selling their land has added an entertainment aspect to their business model to stay solvent.

It appears they have no choice.

They still grow food, but they supplement their income with other gimmicks and activities because they have to grow their business, keep up with their expenses, and stave off the competition.

Our farms become rural amusement parks because the mere act of growing food is somehow not rewarding enough to keep the books in the black, and resting fields become unpaved parking lots where continually growing vehicles degrade the field by compacting the soil.

So just to recap, the land class that grows one of our core essentials is not valued enough by our *humanity bubble* to ensure a decent living wage for those growing that essential.

WTF, mates?

In other cases, the agricultural properties themselves — back to those deeds again, the ones that can now somehow be held by organizational entities and not just individuals — are simply packaged as an investment and traded on markets. There is no shortage of farmland investment vehicles for investors, because expanding into diverse investment options is what we do.

Adding farmland into the investment world sounds great for our portfolios, but what about our dinner plates?

There is an inevitable decline in food quality when farms become one small portion of an immense investment portfolio that requires perpetually increasing returns. Instead of farmers providing food for nourishment, their outputs now serve as the core ingredients of a perpetually expanding variety of low-quality food products aimed at generating income in our *humanity bubble.*

Farm owners must sell their harvest as competitively as possible when forced to keep up with economic growth.

They must entertain to supplement their income.

They must consolidate, just like those brick-and-mortar stores.

They must do what they can to pay their debts, because the food they grow to keep people alive doesn't earn them enough to make a living.

Some stocks grow, others go

Hopefully I'm doing a decent job spreading the systems-speak throughout this book so readers don't bail on me, but we must once more return to the topic.

Stocks.

How much stock is left?

Not the share of a company, but the stockpile of any given resource.

The remaining account balance.

What's left in the warehouse?

Growth can present itself in many forms, but we'll focus on the ill-understood exponential growth, and its oft-ignored opposite: exponential decay. The same exponential growth concept that drives investment compounding drives growth of other things too. Drop a negative sign into all that math and we see decay, the same growth process working in the other direction.

Let's quickly review the monetary example since we know that one best. It's the reason I need you to keep my retirement portfolio humming along.

Your money doesn't appear to be growing that much in the beginning as you are incrementally investing, then it suddenly takes off, hopefully upwards.

You acquire, you retire, then you die. Simple enough.

But the same holds true for non-monetary accumulations. There's a bank for all that other stuff too.

Pollution, for example.

It doesn't seem like much at first. Just a bit of smog from a few factories in the Black Country — whoa, *smog* is actually a combination of smoke and fog! — and a few centuries later we're meeting in Kyoto and then Paris to address our excessive global emissions. Impacts appear minimal to start, but therein lies the danger of compounding, where the initial build-up clandestinely forms the foundation that allows rapid uncontrolled increases later. Nothing changes, until one day there is a spike, and we're like "oh shit, it changed" and it's too late.

Let's randomly consider fish stocks as well, where we'll add a negative sign to our equation.

Decreasing the current fish population by 20 fish each year is trivial. Percentage-wise, the initial impact against the whole population is negligible, but when there are only 40 fish left, removing 20 of them is a 50% decline. The *absolute* decrease of consistently losing 20 fish per year appears benign throughout the experiment — it's also a linear decline from this frame of reference — but the *relative* decrease shifts exponentially as the overall population shrinks. Fish are everywhere, then the end arrives before you can blink.

Where are we now, though? How do we know if there are four billion fish left, or 40?

Who knows?

We don't know the current inventory, and consequently cannot understand the true impact. Millions of fish consistently breeding results in a considerably different replacement rate than a few dozen fish struggling to procreate in the name of their long-term survival, and these aren't just raw materials that we can simply start mining and re-manufacture.

They're living creatures.

We worship this concept of exponents for our investing decisions right here in La La Land, but ignore it with the planet and the very real, very physical stockpiles that affect our ability to live.

That's a choice that we all make, every day.

You can find ways to make more money if your brokerage account hits zero, but we won't be as lucky if our topsoil balance flatlines.

Composting does eventually result in new topsoil, but the true test will be whether we can survive in the months it takes to recreate that absolutely crucial top layer of the earth.

We treat food oddly

Imagine for a moment an astonishing art piece in front of you.

Marvel at the design and creativity of the work, contemplate the labor that went into creating the layers and depth you see before you, admire the deliberately selected colors, and revel in the texture and placement of each element within the arrangement.

Our unique ability to create such art is wonderful, but before you start blabbing about AI's new talents in this creative domain, I have a question for you: Did I just describe artwork in a museum, or food on your plate?

The existence of any mystery whatsoever here indicates a perceived abundance beyond what any other species could ever fathom.

If we as a species have the time, security, and resources to make food into art, and then launch endless reality TV shows about it, then we've got it pretty damn good right now. Our food system amply provides for most of us, but not without ridiculous complexity and some pretty odd requirements. We now have general rules like:

- Thou shalt eat three meals a day, and they shall be named breakfast, lunch, and dinner.

- Thou shalt have those meals at specific times during the day, conveniently in line with that other thing called a work or school day, even if that's not what our body wants.

- Thou shalt assign specific foods to those specific meals, preferably something bread-based at lunch to get us through that work or school day.

- Thou shalt also create snacks and desserts for consumption between these designated meals to hold us over until each mealtime.

- Thou shalt purchase all these items at this oddly titled grocery store.

Every other species just has food, which we've discussed ad nauseum. They seek out something to eat when they are hungry.

That's.

About.

It.

Not us, though. Our supposed security even allows us to eat as a hobby. As an activity in and of itself.

We go out to eat.

We snack out of boredom — the only species able to do that too. We're actually the only species to be bored for that matter.

We eat to be busy.

We eat as an anxiety response.

We eat to feel safe.

We eat to feel better.

We eat to feel *something*.

I have lost track of how many times I abruptly stopped writing and went into the kitchen for a snack.

Sometimes as a result of a breakthrough: "Awesome progress! Spike that dopamine!"

Sometimes because I felt stuck and frustrated: "Damn, I'm stuck, make me happy. Sugary cereal to the rescue!"

But in the end, food is just food. It's energy. It's the nutrients used by our body to function. It's input and output, and just like an engine that runs poorly when we inadvertently fill up at a gas station with bad gas — that's petrol, or gasoline, not that other type of bad gas that some of us release — our bodies likewise perform like garbage with low-quality foods.

In our transition from directly harvesting our essentials out in the natural world to generating food products to be consumed in our *humanity bubble*, we forgot the purpose of eating.

Food is fuel.

We seek fullness and deliciousness, not nourishment, feeling satisfied when our stomachs are at capacity while our unsatiated bodies still crave what they need most.

As long as we are fat and happy, though, what could we possibly need to address here?

Put the donut down for a moment. There is more to discuss regarding this weird relationship we have with our food.

Have you ever seen a fat cheetah?

We have a tendency to portray otherwise lean animals as overweight in pop culture, in all likelihood to make us feel better about the fact that no other species on this planet has the obesity problem we do.

And we have one hell of an obesity problem.

The same way we keep more stuff in our home than we will ever need, we also have more food in our pantries than we could ever require at one time, and more stored energy in our bodies than necessary for our original, natural function.

This obesity problem is unique to our species.

Our domesticated species certainly pack on the kilos too, but we control their food intake and are solely responsible there. I originally planned to use a certain lasagna-loving orange tabby to demonstrate how we portray an otherwise fit animal as fat in our media, but then I remembered how many fat domesticated cats I've actually seen in real life, rendering that example useless.

He may or may not be the only cat consuming lasagna, but he is certainly not alone in the feline obesity department. I'll skip the statistics and simply suggest a day of people-watching.

Muscle mania

We are the only species to somehow have both an excessive fat problem and an excessive muscle problem.

Every other species on this planet has *exactly* the right fat and muscle balance that they need to survive in their natural environment and perform their innate tasks. There are most certainly cases where members of a species are *weaker* than necessary due to scarcity, but they are certainly never *stronger* than needed. They have the right body composition to exist and play their part in the biosphere.

Their muscles strengthen and develop as a byproduct of doing the things they evolved to do, and if not, the weaker ones become prey for another species. It's sad, but those runts that become meals for predators still play a role in the system.

Survival of the fittest.

Only the strong survive.

Circle of life.

Blah blah blah — I'm out of clichés so let's just move along.

We personally grew tired of being a snack for stronger species, so we rewrote the script. We pretty much started our own theater production with this little world-of-make-believe of ours, and now we are the sole species to arbitrarily build muscle as a means of counterbalancing all our unnatural tasks we insist on doing each day.

Other species have no gyms.

No weights.

No tracks.

No protein shakes.

No trainers.

No unnatural movements that we prefer to do in hiding because they keep us in shape but look absurd when doing them.

In a pinch one afternoon I had to do kettlebell swings with a dumbbell. Try that one out and see how that looks in the mirror from the profile view. If you are unfamiliar with the move and are too lazy to search it, think two hands on a dumbbell that you are swinging up and down between your legs as you hinge and then thrust at the hips.

Enjoy that visual.

With our evolution toward an easy, sedentary life, most of us no longer have to rely on the physical strength of our bodies, so our body composition solely depends on the level of effort we wish to dedicate toward strengthening ourselves.

We train our bodies in one way and use them differently in daily life. This concept called *exercise* replaced the physical activity that at one time naturally kept our bodies in their proper shape, and all our newfound free time allows us to maintain musculature that is completely useless and purely aesthetic.

Those silly looking muscle-building moves won't be used for anything other than repeating those same exercises next time, possibly with a heavier weight.

That's what I did the other day. I picked things up, and I put them down right where they came from. The objects ended up back in the same place that they started.

No external work achieved.

When I go out for a run — a rare occurrence these days — I end up right back where I started.

Zero displacement.

No matter how far I go on my bike ride, I always end up right back at my car, where I conveniently load up my bike and sit down to drive back home. Some people even ride bikes in place.

Zero displacement once more.

Strength without purpose — a pursuit in its own right.

Our muscles work, but they no longer *accomplish* any work. Force and displacement and all that fancy physics stuff.

Within our *humanity bubble* that minimizes our physical labor directed solely toward sustaining ourselves, most of us do all our muscles a grave disservice by sitting for nine-plus hours a day completing pointless tasks we've inexplicably deemed important, then attempt to compensate with a concentrated 30-60 minute workout a few days each week to offset the damage. Once more we attempt to be efficient, but it's not the same.

Instead of constant gentle movement throughout the day like our bodies have evolved to support since the Big Fucking Bang, we have been convinced to sit around all day in an idle state, and then attempt to make up for that extensive idleness with an hour or two of intense physical activity thrown in somewhere.

The math might work, but we're missing the unquantifiable. These two graphs are mathematically the same, but that's where their similarity ends.

We'll just use joules as the unit of measure in this graph as an example. The area under both curves may be mathematically equal, but the holistic outcomes are vastly different.

What's a joule, you say? Whew, I'm glad you asked, otherwise this transition would be awkward.

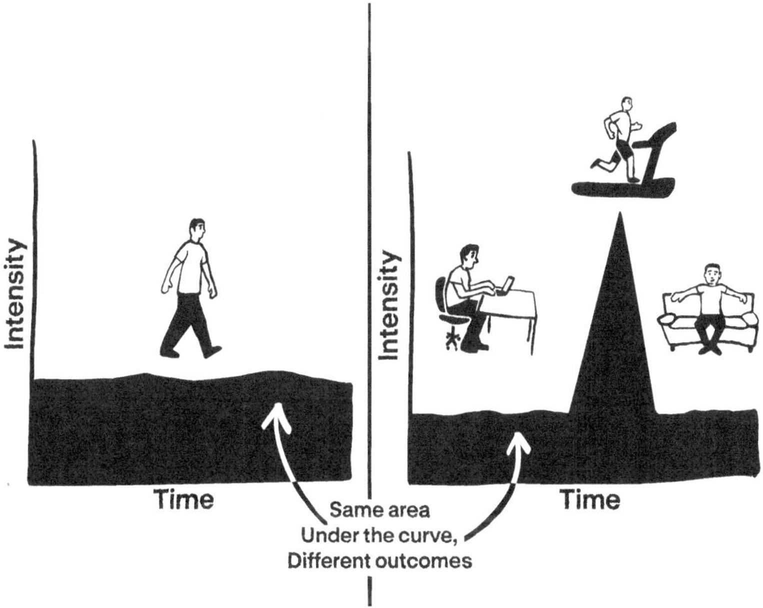

What's a joule?

A joule is simply a unit of energy, and with it we have gamified our lives in the food world.

That's J-O-U-L-E for the audiobook audience I hopefully have the chance to reach. Not to be confused with the jewels on a crown. J-E-W-E-L-S.

We're skipping that imperial unit of measure, calories, but swap them in your head if that's easier. Whichever unit of energy you decide on, no other species is counting them.

No other species *counts*.

Ever the quantifiers, us resourceful humans hijack a unit of measure to help determine how much we should eat.

We set a daily target to either come under, hit exactly, or exceed, depending on our intentions, and then spend each day playing our own unique little game to see where we fall. We even close each day with a daily performance evaluation, conveniently including in our game that direct, immediate feedback we easily recognize and constantly crave.

Remember that basic metabolic rate? The amount of energy you need to burn to keep the lights on, so to speak? That's your bare minimum requirement for staying alive.

If you eat more than that, it needs to go *somewhere*.

You either burn it off, store it in your body, or eject it as waste.

Pretty simple, right?

Unlike that croc in the outback who can survive for a few weeks on what we try to consume daily, we are the only ones who even consider exceeding our daily needs. The daily consumption we consider normal today would have been indicative of royalty centuries ago, back when some humans actually used all those muscles.

That groundhog living under my deck that constantly raids my garden? That was irritating at first, but it doesn't carry any kale off to fill a refrigerator.

That would be silly.

Groundhogs don't have refrigerators.

It takes what it needs at the moment and then comes back for more when it's hungry again, trusting that there will be more available in the garden when it returns.

If not, it looks elsewhere for a meal. No big deal.

My food production out back would be more bountiful if my furry friends allowed a bit of regeneration during the growing season by not eating the *entire* stem of each plant, but I'll work on negotiating that with the groundhog community at a later time.

So, while we continue devising oddly complex food supply solutions, and insisting on solutions we errantly claim are simple like 'just grow more!' — on what land, one might ask, since we keep constructing buildings on the land that grows food — we may want to look at human energy needs with a different lens.

Mind your joules, dudes.

Would you like to see a dessert menu?

I am an addict. A sugar addict.

I grew up drinking a two-liter bottle of soda daily because they were cheaper than substantially smaller-sized soda bottles. That larger soda bottle was also inexplicably cheaper than a half-liter bottle of our liquid essential that we cannot go more than a few days without.

Imagine that.

My portion size for cookies back then was measured by the box, which is about how many cookies I would consume in a single night.

I consume sugar.

Every.

Single.

Day.

I still do.

If you by chance work for the life insurance company that underwrites my policy, please forget what you just read.

My premium is high enough as it is, and I'm pretty sure I just discovered the detrimental indirect effects of refined sugar on LDL cholesterol production. At least that's what the AI thingy told me just after commending me on my efforts to cut my sugar intake.

What a wonderful system, that human body of ours. A body that has no need for the amount of sugar we ingest daily.

No other species eats dessert.

Doggie birthday cakes don't count since we made those and forced them on our canine friends.

Our species has a sugar problem, and the societal norms that drive seemingly innocuous choices throughout our childhood lead us on a decades-long journey later in life to fix the insane sugar habit we unknowingly developed as we aged.

Go to a party, and there will be some sort of cake.

Go out for Halloween — a holiday intended as an annual indulgence — and you are collecting what was once considered a year's worth of candy that kids now consume in a few weeks.

Go to a banquet, there are cookies.

Most grocery stores have bakeries.

Go out to breakfast, lunch, or dinner, and dessert is an option. Even at breakfast?

Yes.

How would you alternatively categorize that stack of chocolate chip pancakes with syrup and strawberry sauce and whipped cream and sprinkles? Ever check the sugar content of most yogurt products?

Last summer we had donuts in the office three times in a single week to celebrate multiple concurrent milestones.

Why donuts?

I have no idea. It's just somehow the thing we buy to celebrate professionally, and I wish at least one of those people chose an ornamental fruit basket instead. I'll add that to their next performance review.

What was once merely sustenance, an essential source of nourishment, has become a luxury.

A hobby.

A profession.

An entertainment piece that plays to the desire of our taste buds at the expense of our stomachs.

 Be right back, snack break.

Tastebud Takeover

Okay, where were we? Right, taste buds.

Let's talk about the human tongue. What nasty, slithering, conniving little snakes our tongues have become.

It is an anatomical tool of ours that evolved to help detect things that would kill us if consumed, but it has now been weaponized against us to subconsciously choose a manufactured poison over the good stuff. My aforementioned sugar addiction is probably something you are dealing with as well, and a consequence of our tongues tricking us.

We have unknowingly delegated our eating decisions to our taste buds, with society steering us toward options that take advantage of this relatively recently rewired internal circuitry of ours.

I will subjectively claim that 90% of the products in the grocery stores I frequent here in the U.S. are at best useless, and at worst harmful to our health, yet our taste buds lead the way to those aisles, convincing us to eat larger than necessary quantities of food products that provide minimal nutritional benefit to our bodies.

We had no choice earlier in our human existence, as we ate what we could find or we starved.

We now decided to get clever, since our mono-species decision on land ownership, coupled with a bit of free time, leads us to believe our resource inventory is infinite.

Too clever for our own good.

Even when your stomach has had enough and it's ready to explode, your tongue will still tell you to ingest more, clearly ignoring the fullness signal emanating from your gut. It takes the negative sensation of a stomach-ache to outweigh the positive feedback of the tongue's excitement for you to realize you need to stop, at which point you've already overdone it.

We are so hooked on certain foods that we try to combine healthy ingredients in a way that mimics our favorite foods:

Hamburgers made of beets that taste like a burger.

Chicken fingers made of soy or wheat that we hope will taste like chicken.

Pizza crust made of cauliflower.

Just eat the beets! Just eat the soy or wheat! Just eat the caulif…. meh, cauliflower is optional. No one really likes plain cauliflower anyway.

Statements like 'That was delicious!' or 'That was a terrible meal' describe the taste aspect of a meal. They are sensory reactions from our good ol' friend the tongue. Unfortunately, the phrase 'I feel nourished' doesn't really roll off the tongue, and based on our tongue's newfound allegiance to shit foods, those words would never reach our lips.

Keep it simple

Food shouldn't be fun.

Sorry.

I know we love our food, and it should absolutely be delicious, but we are mere children looking for entertainment in the kitchen.

Adults somehow still play with their food like toddlers but excuse it as creative. The funny face drawn in mashed potatoes as a child signifies the makings of a critically acclaimed baking show contestant in adulthood trying to create an edible leather boot because why not.

Our belief that humans could develop a better food system than what has supported us for our entire existence is very —well— human of us.

Quite frankly, that checks out on the arrogance meter.

Ever wonder why most produce has no advertising? As much as I'd like to chide the marketing community for being inept at making kale seem appealing, it simply sells itself to those that get it.

We can very easily prepare base ingredients and then flavor them with seasonings instead of processing them into a marketable product. Boring food doesn't mean tasteless food: it just takes time and money that unfortunately most of us don't have.

Those marketable food products are easier, and the *point of receipt* deceives us. We see our simple workload and look no further at the immense production processes throughout the rest of the system.

We are energy-inefficient eaters, consuming overcomplicated, processed concoctions of random ingredient combinations instead of throwing all the raw essentials into a pot and calling it a day.

We have been convinced food is hard when in fact those five senses of ours evolved to help us eat. We just have to use those senses to guide us, but they are at the moment distracted by all of the other fun toys in our lives, while the resources we should make abundant — those essentials that past ancestors could easily find — disappear.

And if you randomly feel hungry after reading this, I will pester my dear readers as I pester my child.

Drink more of the thing you can't live a few days without until your pee runs clear, *then* consume the thing you can go weeks without.

Speaking of pee!...

We mandate where we relieve ourselves

And now a quick conversation about where we go to the bathroom.

It should be a rather benign discussion, I would think. Nothing potentially contentious about this topic at all.

It's just poop and pee, but how many rules, regulations, and laws exist at all levels of government that dictate where we perform these primal bodily functions? Not to mention the social norms we apply on top of our legally binding rules.

Important government people in charge of other serious matters actually took time out of their day to deliberate this topic, and they somehow expect us all to take them seriously.

Your tax dollars at work.

No species has set out to control biological relief quite like we have. More simply put, no other species gives a shit about where they shit like we do.

Perhaps we would be having a different conversation if the males in other species had their own newspapers and smartphones and wanted to hide from their families, but here we are, standing — or more likely sitting — in solidarity on this issue.

Every other species on this planet merely goes when they gotta go, wherever they happen to be. Sometimes they don't even stop moving.

They basically just go while they're walking.

Or swimming.

Or flying.

Has anyone else ever gotten hit by falling poop from the sky? 'Good luck' is how we rationalize it.

Doubtful.

Fucking birds.

Go when ya gotta go, though. I support that thought process, in theory at least. Our domesticated friends do as well.

Pets try to emulate their wild brethren by going wherever they are when they have to go, until of course we correct them. We tell them they need to relieve themselves in certain places, and while their instinct disagrees, we as the masters of all creatures, great and small, win out with those we control.

We chastise them for going in the wrong place. We get angry at them when they pee on our carpet, or on the leg of our chair. Or in the cages we lock them in for extended periods while we are away.

In some cases, it actually surprises us. How can they do this, we say?

To which I say, we are the weird ones, us and our porcelain thrones.

We claim intellectual superiority over other species, but that dumb puppy actually has it right. We'd sooner alter our own anatomy for the drive out to Long Island than accept that we should just go when nature calls. Apparently, bladder surgeries for people in traffic are a thing.

Who knew?

I will once more suggest that simply spending less time in the car is the more sensible solution here, but I'm not hopeful since it's more likely we'd add a toilet to our cars than decide to use our vehicles less.

Alright, that's enough fun for now. Let's get on to the more serious part of this shitty conversation.

Our waste, a wasted resource

Species that go to the bathroom wherever they are at any given moment are contributing to a natural cycle that we disrupted in our *humanity bubble*.

I bet you never referred to what you leave in the bathroom as a resource, have you? *Especially* given the mess some of us leave behind in there. I've done my fair share of damage here, sorry, everyone!

A resource it is, though. Ever hear of manure?

Even though we flush it all down the drain and send it *over there*, we still somehow manage to isolate it from the rest of the world once it leaves our homes.

Our innovative waste treatment solutions are impressive, but here we are again devising an intricate answer to a non-problem that already has a natural solution in place since we started roaming the earth.

Humans have used some form of plumbing for ages, with more advanced and widespread use ramping up a few hundred years ago. That timeframe is sufficient to normalize these waste management practices in the minds of our current generations who don't know any better, but realistically speaking, our plumbing mastery has only been in place for a small fraction of our overall existence.

Why don't we just leave that shit alone for the earth to reclaim?

Yikes.

Imagine the assault on our senses if we just let loose like that?

It's almost like we require such an elaborate waste management system due to our excessively large but somehow not-invasive-species-level population numbers.

At any rate, please don't start going wherever you please. This is a thought exercise.

Just think about the difference between waste evenly distributed across the planet versus present-day concentrated disposal methods. That waste was doing something, and then we changed the resource flow.

We can conclude easily enough that *something* changed.

What's the big deal?

Who cringed when I mentioned bowel movements a few pages back?

It's laughable how self-conscious we are with our bodily functions.

A small detriment of this crazy mind of ours, along with the relative comfort we seek within our *humanity bubble*. Even with a semi-permeable boundary, we still don't want anything that smells too strongly in there.

Never mind the disgust we feel if we ever come into external contact with something that literally just came out of the inside of us.

Gross.

Parents get it, though, especially those who have removed a diaper off their baby boy without immediately deploying proper tent coverage.

We do everything we can to ensure our waste makes it into an enclosed or submerged container or vessel.

We try to hold it at every turn, and we don't dare deviate from our norms, since in certain circumstances we could end up dealing with extreme legal consequences by freely doing our business in that wooded area we fail to realize is right next to a school playground.

There is no greater self-inflicted torture than not being allowed to go when you urgently have to go.

I remember stopping at a highway rest stop one summer and the line to use the women's room extended out the restroom itself and snaked throughout the building. I thought nothing of it as I casually walked into the men's room within seconds of arriving, but on my way out I passed a young girl bouncing up and down in place, telling her mother that she really had to go. Based on the length of the line she probably had another 15 minutes or so.

Such a shame, especially for our nascent offspring. Think of our upbringing. In earlier years, we went as we pleased in that cloth thing wrapped around our bodies.

Whenever.

Wherever.

It didn't matter.

We were free to pee as we pleased until we hit an age where we should suddenly know better. An age at which we transitioned to finding relief in specific places at specific times.

A logical progression that toddlers couldn't possibly misconstrue.

My crazy suggestion in the last chapter about consuming water until our pee runs clear is untenable, because we spend the first few decades of life in an education system that harshly controls *when* we go just as much as *where* we go.

From the moment we leave diapers to the moment we receive our college diplomas — or decide on other perfectly legitimate yet conveniently unmentioned alternative routes that don't get as much attention as university — we are taught to ask permission to relieve ourselves, and this restriction can even extend further into life depending on post-educational employment.

I guess we just have to wait until we hit senior age and we can return to where we all started, donning shit-filled diapers once more.

Yes, we *can* hold it, but in all of our muscular strengthening, why do we insist on strengthening our sphincter muscles by holding it so much?

Hold it just one more minute

I've repeatedly mentioned throughout this book that I am not pushing for immediate action, and that point bears repeating here in particular. While this section has absolutely nothing to do with my retirement accounts, there is definitely nothing you need to do about this one right now.

I repeat, immediate action is not required.

I simply ask that you spend some time pondering the stark difference between these two thought processes:

Every other species:

Proceeds to just go without a thought

Humans:

"I gotta go. Where's the toilet?"

We alter our appearance

We are aesthetics-based decision makers.

An overwhelming majority of our decisions revolve around some version of: "How does it *look*?" Feel free to swap *look* with *smell*, *sound*, *feel*, or *taste* if you wish, since we do the same thing with the other senses.

In general, if it doesn't look appealing, smell pleasant, sound pleasing, feel comfortable, or taste delectable, we reject it. Our five senses, now the snooty arbiters of opulence that guide our way through this world.

The rest of the species on this planet are survival-based decision makers, dealing with questions like:

- Can I eat it?

- Can it eat me?

- Will it kill me just for the hell of it?

- Can I sleep here?

- Should I stay?

- Should I go?

We operate freely and safely within our bubble, while others are constantly functioning in survival mode. They might get eaten if they so much as stop and look in the mirror.

Mirror, mirror, on every wall

We seem to have taken to heart the words of a well-known fairy tale mirror that proclaims to tell us who looks best.

It's probably unrelated, but we all worry about our appearance now.

We are the only species with mirrors *everywhere*. With the exception of a few truck stops, every bathroom in the developed world has one.

We put them randomly in rooms throughout our house. One place even had a large mirror on the bedroom ceiling! What could they possibly nee... oh...

...right.

There are endless reflective surfaces randomly strewn about our artificial world. We keep them in our pockets at this point too, thanks to our smartphones and the advent of the forward-facing camera that lets us check our teeth after a meal.

Other species see their reflection and freak out because they don't realize it is themselves that they see. They see danger and instinctively flee or attack.

As we constantly admire, critique, evaluate, judge, and shame, we continue to alter ourselves to look the way we *think* we should look, whatever that means.

Elective surgeries.

Collagen fillers.

Anti-aging creams.

Exfoliants.

Other skin-care treatments.

Entire stores dedicated to enhancing your appearance that I personally cannot enter due to their overwhelming aromas.

I recently walked by an office of an M.D. with a degree in Aesthetics.

My general practitioner's office has flyers everywhere for appearance-enhancing procedures that aim to boost our confidence. I am here because I am sick; I don't need to be bombarded with advertisements about laser skin care treatments to look good at the beach.

How's your skin, by the way? Nice and tan? Every other species that sunbathes does it for temperature regulation. Skin cancer be damned, we want to look good!

You know who doesn't get skin cancer? Iguanas.

I conveniently learned about cosmetic centers on the road last month. Not from the radio or a podcast, but instead from the back of a dump truck. Butt lifts, mommy makeovers, abdominal etching. Numerous options prominently advertised on the back of a large construction vehicle for all to see.

Yes, the kids see it too, who may not consciously understand the message but will subconsciously absorb it and other examples of our society relentlessly impressing the importance of looks on them.

Those muscles we talked about?

At one time meant for achieving meaningful work, they now simply look good in a tank top. I can say with confidence at least one human on the planet has exercised their muscles for aesthetic reasons, and that human was me ~~in my 20s~~ right now. I almost tried to imply that I ceased that vain behavior, but self-awareness is important!

See if you can walk by a reflective surface without looking at yourself.

I sure can't.

Who else has hair salons?

"I think I can use milkshake but I'm going to go to cover, I don't think a five will be too...

...If you went to five and cover, you'd be fine, if you went to six and milkshake that may be too much."

I don't know what that quote means.

I heard some combination of those words at a hair salon once, so while I may have botched the order a bit, there are apparently real terms sprinkled in there somewhere.

I went from "WTF are they saying?!?!?" to "Oh damn I should write this down for my book!" as fast as I could, but it might as well have been a foreign language to me. I definitely couldn't tell you what was happening, but someone was getting *that* done to their hair.

Humans have altered their hair forever, and not just the hair on our heads. We have laser hair removals, shavers, bikini waxes, wigs, and toupees. Manscaping is even a thing, and don't you dare let those grey ear hairs get too long, guys!

A few methods exist to *add* hair, but we'll ignore those, and my bald-ish head, for now.

Plenty of hair coloring options exist as well, as we insist on restoring it to its original condition instead of acknowledging that greying hair is nothing more than an indication that we pushed our lifespans beyond what evolution had planned for us.

All of this hairy nonsense is what leaves us myriad years later as the only species replacing their natural body covering with clothing. In accordance with our *humanity bubble* norms, we've also adopted the clean-shaven look as the standard professional appearance, and anyone with a massive beard is labeled either a metalhead, a ren faire aficionado, or someone stuck in an archaic time.

We even support this narrative with our portrayal of our distant ancestors in the media, where that dude's beard is too damn squared off and perfectly trimmed for 1546. Same with his cleanly shaven washboard abdominal muscles — those are way too perfect.

Then you have the fools like me who shave their head clean-ish but grow a beard. What can I say? It looks good, and my beard keeps my face warm in the winter, remember?

Other species don't have barber shops or salons, although we did create them for certain animals. We groom, cut, or shear all those sheep, dogs, cats, and alpacas for various reasons, but they could never make a salon on their own.

We expend finite resources to look good. To remold ourselves in *someone's* image.

I'd say God's image, but I can't confirm that the great deity of ours residing upstairs has a mirror there.

We depend on technology to reproduce

We are the only species utilizing hospitals to support reproduction.

That's all I will say for this one.

I cry for a week after stubbing my toe, I grumble when my knees act up every four days, and I could fill an entire complaint department with my whining whenever I experience any other injury.

You would think the world was ending whenever I simply get up off the couch, so I'm wading no deeper into the stormy waters of pregnancy and childbirth.

Not here, not ever.

Moms, you are *fucking heroes*.

I cannot comprehend how you do it, and this world would fall apart without you.

Readers can compare our intricate, medically-assisted birthing process with the simple, more natural version every other species adopts outside of our isolated *humanity bubble*, and independently evaluate how that might be detrimental to our long-term survival.

Before moving on, please call your mom to say hello and tell her you love her if you are still fortunate enough to have the opportunity.

We extend our lifespan

By 19th century standards I should be dead right now.

Fortunately, human life expectancy has miraculously doubled since then, which in theory confirms I am experiencing a mid-life break right now and not an end-of-life break.

It's just a break, remember?

Not a crisis.

Unfortunately, as great as that may sound for our individual lifespans, it doesn't bode well for our longevity as a species.

The lifespan of every other species on the planet has essentially remained flat over the same time.

The only other species to have any meaningful slope change in their life span would be those species we killed off, and their line drops off as precipitously as the cliff we metaphorically pushed them off.

We once more have our ingenuity to thank for our newfound human longevity. Advances in science, medicine, sanitation, hygiene, and general health have led to longer lives for us *Homo sapiens*.

This is all wonderful news.

I am personally thrilled that I am not dead right now.

I'm thankful I can still see despite my terrible eyesight.

I'm excited that I still have teeth to chew my delicious food, despite my excessive sugar consumption.

I'm grateful my heart is still beating, also despite my excessive sugar consumption.

I am fortunate my bones are not fragile.

These are all great things, and I hope they never change for future generations, but behind all this wonderful advancement I can't help but wonder if we have grossly outpaced all of the internal and external supporting infrastructure that makes human life possible on the planet in the first place.

Longer living makes for a happy you and me, but it also necessitates more food, energy, and resources for each individual human life, and living into our 90s also requires additional medical care, since the evolution of the human body has not kept up.

Our societal insistence on measuring the success of our lives by maximum net worth instead of minimal resource usage also means we rarely concern ourselves with how much we consume.

Of all the games to play that involve keeping the score as low as possible, the resource usage game is the one we should play.

The earth actuaries did not plan for that

Our planet slowly evolved over eons to support humans that lived two to four decades. All of a sudden, at least from the perspective of the planet, we live almost a century.

Sometimes longer.

That shift requires a lot of additional resources, and as we know based on that whole conservation of matter thing, we allegedly can't create new matter, so the resources to supply food, housing, and other goods for our longer lives must come from the existing planetary stockpile. Coupled with the minor fact that there are simply more of us on the planet at any given time now, the earth cannot keep up with our resource usage.

Even without being excessive, the standard consumption rate alone by the sheer number of humans on this earth is stressing the system.

It's like two people packed supplies for a four-day camping trip and ended up out in the wilderness for three years, and the expedition suddenly and inexplicably grew to 10,000 members.

The group quickly consumes the planned supplies, and then it's time to improvise.

We are crushing it in improvise mode right now, but our skill in this department regrettably masks the frantically reactive state we find ourselves in today. The catastrophe looms unnoticed because someone engineers a solution just in time, every time.

In theory, the earth would naturally adjust to meet the rising demand, but our progress shot up asymptotically.

We grew too damn fast. The benefits of being the dominant species with no predators, I suppose.

Given all our planning in other facets of *humanity bubble* life, such as the instructions I received in my 20s to start my retirement planning, I remain astounded that we still operate on the baseless assumption that endless resources will just keep coming from *over there*.

The planet hasn't caught up yet, and isn't ready to support the significantly increased consumption of twice as many humans living twice as long and being ten times as gluttonous.

Our race to outrun evolution

We walk this earth much longer than before, and much like the planet, our bodies themselves are also struggling to keep up.

I am no anatomist, but it appears we have outpaced the natural evolution that our bodies would otherwise undergo to ensure key organs can support these longer lifespans. We have increased our lifespan so aggressively that we simply outlast certain body parts now.

We're blitzkrieging so hard in our war against death that our tank formations have outrun the resupply convoy.

Dentures and dental implants are innovative masterpieces, but have you ever thought of why we need them in the first place?

While I must admit that plenty of us die in old age with a beautiful set of teeth, generally speaking we now outlast our teeth by decades. Teeth are susceptible to damage for a multitude of reasons — sugar addicts like me eventually need help either way — but one reason could plausibly be that they just haven't evolved to last as long as our hearts can now keep beating.

Sometimes the heart itself stops beating, a chamber fails, or an artery clogs, but we have concocted a way to fix those. In some extreme cases we even put someone else's heart in the failed one's place.

Forever pushing limits in all facets of life, we likewise push our bodies to their working limits with our great innovations, conducting organ-by-organ repairs or replacements to squeeze out the years.

Bone density issues, brain deterioration, loose skin, joint failure, hair loss, arterial plaque buildup, low A1C, eyesight loss, psoriasis. We have a solution for all of it. If you're in the U.S. — the only place on the planet where it's apparently necessary for patients to tell doctors what medications they need — you've seen the ads for solutions to all of it.

A natural, evolutionary change in the human body typically takes — I don't know — a very long time?

Yet we doubled our lifespan in a few centuries — maybe five human generations? I'm pretty sure evolution needs *a lot* longer than the 150 years of our recent growth spurt to catch up, which suggests that our true human life expectancy in the natural world is still that same two to four decades it always was, we've just artificially extended it within our *humanity bubble.*

Fighting for minutes after wasting the years

A centenarian that plays an active role in their community is a pleasure. If any of them are as unfiltered and carefree as some of the elderly I know, then they're just a hoot. Just think about all those blue-zone peeps living their best carefree lives out there.

An older individual that is an incoherent vegetable permanently occupying a hospital bed, however, is merely a cash flow generator for the care facility and other third parties. Someone is racking up points as grandma lies there waiting to die.

As we say, though, all lives matter, and we must do everything we can to fight death, regardless of the quality of life achieved in the fight. Leave it to humans to inanely and arrogantly throw vast resources to delay death, the one true inevitability in this world.

Why do we extend life as long as possible?

My immediate snarky answer would be that longer life equals more money for someone else and that we've all just been hoodwinked into yearning for our very own *old age high score*, but the more pressing concern we need to consider is how our inability to live our best lives in our core years drives us to desperately pursue more time at the end.

We are by law shoved into school at five years old and stay there for a few decades, depending on our respective paths, and from there we have the honor of spending another two to four decades working.

Consider how the masses are promoted into a comfortable middle-class life by the global war on poverty no one asked for in the name of economic opportunity — that whole 'penetrating global markets' stragery — only to be trapped on that rung of the demographic ladder by the presence of all that disposable income and the blatant lack of a similar crusade to elevate us to the next rung.

Where's the middle-class escape plan promoting us into the next societal echelon?

We merrily grant ourselves the right to wait until 60 to finally be free, and thank someone for the privilege. When we don't get to do what we want for the first 50-70 years of our *entire lives*, of course we're going to want every minute we can in our retirement. What a crazy revelation, realizing that people would want to do what *they* want for the majority of their time on this earth.

How fucking selfish of us.

Our sense of entitlement to a long life — our demand for more of that nebulous stuff called time — stems from nothing more than a fear of dying before truly living. Maybe if we devoted the majority of our lives to doing what we *want* to do, life would be more fulfilling and we wouldn't push to extend it in perpetuity.

Tell that to your bosses, and let me know how that goes.

We do life wrong, and it is time for change. I have attended too many retirement parties over the past five years and I don't like what I've seen. I actually ran into one of those retirees at a ball game a few months after their party and they never seemed happier, smiling ear to ear and bouncing with positive energy. A far cry from the last time I saw them in the office, when they were a stressed out, anxious mess.

I personally refuse to wait until the end of life to feel sustained joy.

Get the most out of each day, and you can say with pride on your death bed that you took advantage of the time you had.

That you carpe diem'ed hard.

That you YOLO'ed the shit out of this one life you had.

I have no desire to die right now. I would really like to not die at all, but given the unlikeliness of that hope and dream, I'll ask: When is the right time to die? How old is too old?

Don't worry about it.

Enjoy today.

Remember we die, and as those around us inevitably succumb to death, we have other unique traditions that extend beyond the grave.

We obsess over the dead

Humans have a perplexing relationship with death.

We honor the fallen, remember those we've lost, and indelibly etch them in our memory.

Other species probably don't even notice. "Hey, where's Fred today? Has anyone seen him? Oh well, let's keep moving. Winter is coming!" Their companions die, and they simply move on without a second thought. The carcass simply decomposes or is eaten by scavengers.

No land required for post-death practices, as far as I can tell.

Have you ever seen another species organizing a funeral?

I mean, I have a hunch that every other species is clandestinely and joyously preparing for the funeral of humanity, but you never see them organizing one for their own kind.

Death enables the mere recirculation of resources contained within a once living organism. A resource transfer. An exchange of the elements from one form to another.

"IT'S THE CIRCLE...!!!"

Just kidding. No one needs to hear me singing.

Driven by a multitude of factors like our religions, our belief in an afterlife, and whatever other rituals we have adopted, humans have obstructed the resource recirculation process.

We are sentimental. We hold on, and we continuously advance the ways in which we hold on. Forever.

Some keep mementos.

Some make shrines.

Others put those 'in memoriam' decals on their vehicles.

We already mentioned cemeteries and the land they occupy. As a reminder, most of the deceased are still landowners, and we inexplicably seem okay with that premise.

Will the 50-year mark be when my dead grandfather finally gives up his claim to land?

Probably not. It will be eternity.

Once more our evolved and unoccupied brains disrupt the natural order by overcomplicating an otherwise simple process. We've so strongly stigmatized disturbing the dead that nothing short of world war or societal collapse would convince us to repurpose those areas.

At the end of the day, we are all just big bags of hydrogen, oxygen, carbon, and microplastics, all of which eventually rejoin the earth.

From our mothers we are grown, and back to Mother Earth we eventually return at the end of it all.

At least that's what should happen.

Robbing our future to honor the past

Organic matter, or 'dead stuff' as some may prefer to call it, replenishes our ecological systems.

Simple enough.

Yes, that means those distant ancestors that we now lock in coffins were once an amazing source of fertilizer.

From a biological perspective, there is no significant difference in the decomposition process of a fallen tree, a deer that had an unfortunate run-in with a truck, and a human body that roams no more. Human bodies are biodegradable in the same way leftover plant matter decomposes to help feed us.

Our decision to go another way probably has something to do with us vehemently refusing to eat grandma's decomposed remains, even though there is a complete chemical breakdown and molecular rearrangement of the elements that renders her unrecognizable.

Nope. We chose other options.

Sometimes we burn the bodies, allowing the atoms to rejoin the world in a different, less efficient means. Maybe the ashes end up somewhere, but I don't think breathing in the remains of your loved ones as they leave the crematorium exhaust stack really helps. All that remains within the furnace doesn't help either, as we typically keep that in an urn on our mantel.

Our permanent subterranean lodging practices are so isolating that the term *pushing up daisies*, a common phrase used for someone who recently died, has no true meaning anymore, since nutrients from dead bodies no longer reach the surface in a timely manner to feed the plants above.

Boxes more luxurious than some 19th century dwellings seal up bodies and severely delay nutrient absorption by the planet, and even if bodies once more pushed up wildflowers, we would just spray them with weed killer to maintain those impeccable cemetery lawns.

We certainly don't want dead bodies everywhere, and I suppose having bags of synthetic fertilizer readily available at a hardware store for purchase and immediate application makes more sense than selling a biodegradable body bag that would take a decade or so to fully break down.

The fertilizer approach works better — we're always in a rush.

As we stubbornly continue our nonsensical practice in the name of tradition, we cannot even plead ignorance regarding the benefits of giving our bodies back to the land. Movies and shows portraying a post-apocalyptic community typically involve the cast burying a fallen comrade in their farms to replenish the nutrients of the field.

In other more arid settings, the people reclaim a body's water or nutrients for the good of the community.

When resources appear sparse, we magically drop the charade blinding us in our *humanity bubble* and forego all tradition and ceremony to keep ourselves alive, but when resources appear abundant we just don't seem to have any interest in proactively taking this clearly sensible approach.

To be fair, some cultures might, but I refuse to conduct any research on the topic.

As vile as my internet search history already is, I refuse to add 'Does anyone bury dead human bodies on a farm?' to that data set. Some topics are a line too far, so I'll just assume there's at least one human tribe out there doing things right.

Those of us in the modern world understand the mechanics behind resource recirculation, but assumed abundance renders that level of conservation unnecessary.

We simultaneously know it takes time to nurture fertile land, yet also forget that this lag is another reason we shouldn't act the way we do. We cannot wait for the proverbial 'oh shit!' moment to arrive before we start composting grandma and grandpa. Regeneration takes time, and they conveniently skip that part in the movies. They bury the body, and in the very next scene we see an entire garden.

That's not exactly reflective of reality.

We continuously take from the earth, then selfishly hoard the resources that we took within our bodies beyond death, and our inability to let go of the past is preventing us from giving those resources back to the system for the good of the future.

Death doesn't even free us from financial liability in our *humanity bubble*, with our insistence on charging each other a nominal body disposal fee while we deny Mother Nature access to our resources.

You can't just die anymore. You have to pay an exit tax.

But hey, at least the funeral business is steady.

Well played, monetizing that one inevitability in life.

Projecting our obsession onto our pets

There are companies that can create a custom stuffed animal of your pet.

There are also companies that will stuff your dead pet. Yes, the actual corpse of your dead companion.

Assuming this wasn't a fake post, it appears you can keep Spot next to the end table forever, and if he was large enough in life, he could *be* your end table in death.

Do you know anyone with ashes of their pet?

I still have at least one urn with a dead dog somewhere, as well as a red rubber ball that one of them played with. I'm also pretty sure one of my jacket sleeves still has a drool stain on it from one of my pups that I refused to clean, because it was from the last time I saw her alive.

So, I get it.

We do weird things to honor our dead, human or otherwise. I found a dead bee on my deck once and ceremoniously buried the poor lil' guy in my compost pile.

Instead of confronting cultural traditions and instilling some pragmatism in our lives, we instead opt once more to project our unnatural practices onto other species.

These other animals don't care, though.

They instinctively wander off as the end approaches, seeking out a peaceful, isolated death. Their brains can't fabricate the death-related nonsense we dream up in our spare time, and they own no things that they must pass along through a will.

Let them go in peace, and grant yourself peace by properly grieving, then letting them go.

Projecting our obsession onto our possessions

We make great things.

We saw them all as we looked around at the start of this book.

We are a proud species, and we of course take pride in these great things we make. So proud in fact that when we make something really great, we attempt to preserve it forever. We lock those resources up for eternity, and expend even more resources to maintain these treasures in a preserved state.

We refuse to let our *things* die — that's next-level maintenance.

We keep creations from bygone eras intact and in functional condition, then gawk at them in large buildings that are in some cases themselves also artifacts.

Ever been to a museum?

What are those, you ask?

You probably don't ask, since most of us took at least one school field trip to a museum as a child, but I'm once more taking advantage of my last name and rewriting a definition to another common word:

Museums are human inanimate object cemeteries.

We proudly maintain our past innovations in these buildings, applying our false sense of permanence onto our creations, similar to how we treat our bodies in their coffins.

Hands off our resources!

The items that survive the test of time are our truest failures as we perpetuate their existence in defiance of that pesky law of impermanence, and the cost of maintenance increases with age as we push the limits of that law.

One museum full of items seems inconsequential, but consider how many buildings full of non-functional artifacts exist, and the volume of the world they occupy that is now maintained at very precise environmental conditions.

End of the line

Don't cancel your school field trips just yet, and don't dump grandma's corpse out back when she passes either.

Remember, this book is a thought exercise, and just like our critique of other bodily functions, we close yet another topic by emphasizing that no immediate action is required.

I merely encourage you to ponder the basic essence of life and death — nothing too intellectually taxing at all.

Maybe there's an afterlife, or we just become dust in the end.

Maybe we go to heaven.

If you're like me, you're on the wrong side of heaven and on the way to hell, where I assuredly have a reservation in the 5th ring. That level of hell has all the angry peeps, right? That's probably a good fit.

Maybe it just goes dark for eternity.

Nobody knows. We'll probably never know.

If only an equation could explain death, then perhaps we could solve the mystery, but until then we just simply wait and see.

We obsess over death.

We bury our dead in ways that render resources and land inaccessible from the rest of the world's natural systems.

We subject our domesticated companions and prized material possessions to similar treatment.

What folly then, that even in death, hidden under the guise of tradition and ceremony, we in our final act selfishly withhold from the biosphere.

Our Future as a Species

The earth will be fine

I have no interest in saving the planet.

Regardless of what we do as a species, this planet isn't going anywhere, and to so arrogantly believe lil' ol' humanity could end a planet is laughable.

There is one theory — the more likely one — that says a big bang started this all, but even the biggest bang we could possibly make with our nukes and MOABs wouldn't make this rock flinch.

She'll be fine.

Mother Nature is resilient, her longevity is inevitable, and she'll brush that human bullshit off her shoulder like the gnat of a species that we are.

She is not going anywhere so long as that bright star in the sky keeps burning.

She is also not competing.

She just acts naturally.

She maintains balance.

We do not.

If we were to visualize imbalance by species, everyone else would be harmoniously interacting with the earth while we're flying off into space.

Despite our relentless assault on the natural world, our impacts will dissipate long after we are gone.

Our razing and remolding of the earth's surface, painful as it is to see now, will eventually subside. We'll either come to our senses and relieve the tension, or that rubber band of ours will snap and we'll vanish from this earth before we see the rebalance take place.

Even the most barren of land that we strip of all vegetation will eventually regrow *something* when left unperturbed. You saw this growth in action if you completed that peculiar yard work I assigned you earlier.

Hundreds of those abandoned properties, those superfund sites heavily polluted with hazardous materials — and coincidentally the same type of site that destroyed my local drinking water supply — will self-remedy in time.

The terraced quarries of our abandoned mining operations closely resemble riverside cliffs boasting vineyards elsewhere on the planet, a glimmer of hope for those spaces as well.

Our landfills, terrible as they are, merely form the beginnings of mineral-laden mountains for future species to hopefully not excavate and mine millennia from now. Anything we throw into them, no matter what form, will eventually break down into one of those 118 elements in existence on this planet, deposited randomly in successive layers.

Like roots through a walkway, the earth will eventually prevail, rejecting our *humanity bubble* and restoring some semblance of natural order.

You just have to be on the right timescale to understand.

Mother Nature's timescale of eons extends well beyond our century-long timeline of a human life, our pithy quarter-year scales, and weekly calendars that we swear by. She shrugs off the decomposition of those foam cups we constantly worry about.

With enough time the natural equilibrium of the world restores itself.

Whether or not we are here to witness that equilibrium remains to be seen. I said a future *species* could potentially mine those landfills-turned-mountains in a few millennia, not future *humans*.

The planet will carry on.

Our friends will be fine

I also have zero interest in saving our fellow species.

They don't need any human intervention whatsoever, and they would certainly benefit from us ceasing all our shitty treatment of them. They're following the script of real life by remaining in balance with the planet, securing themselves a place at the table in the post-human era.

They are doing just fine despite our constant evisceration of their populations. They don't envy us. There is no "meeting of the non-human minds" where they all clamor to join us in our *humanity bubble*.

Who in their right mind would want our complicated lifestyle?

I sure don't, but lacking any other viable options, I am resigned to remain.

Other species don't have the reasoning ability to even consider living the way we do, and they don't hoard resources or pretend to have the reserves necessary to sustain such a lifestyle.

They just go about their day. Sometimes they die. Sometimes they live to see another day. A spider spins its web, a fox digs a burrow, a monkey throws poo, and a bird eats seeds.

Their likelihood of survival may seem questionable to us — we certainly put them at a severe disadvantage — but we are simply training them to outlast us. They are weak when navigating human fantasyland, but out in the real world they are fully capable.

They are just as resilient as the earth they call home. They are wild, and they sure as hell don't need our help.

We're [probably] doomed

Our sole concern should be the future of *our* species.

Duh — the book title?

My generation will die off as expected. Our biggest threat right now is staying current with all this new technology, said every aging generation ever.

Our descendants two to three generations from now will also be fine. We'll innovate our way through the next century or so, and then those elusive and poorly understood consequences will start to appear through the cracks.

After that, who knows?

I refer you back one last time to the book title, and how you knew where this discussion was going from the start.

In our minds the giants of the earth, our species is realistically nothing more than a pesky gnat annoyingly flying around Mother Nature's face. Annoying enough to be noticed, but too small to be given any real attention right now.

As we continue to swarm her, though, she starts with subtle hints to cut the crap, similar to how we casually wave our hands near our faces to shoo off bothersome insects.

She'll summon the wind and rain, degrade our food supply, drop the earth out from under us with a few sinkholes, maybe send a tsunami or two, and erupt a few volcanoes around the globe. She may even turn up the heat a bit to sweat out the virus, whatever she must do until it comes time to finally rid herself of the misbehaving anomaly.

Translation: she'll eventually smash us.

She may cause some collateral damage as she smacks herself in the process, but she will heal.

The gnat is not as lucky.

That's us. We're the gnat, not the giant. We are the target, and things will escalate from *life is peachy* to *dead* without warning.

Giants without question according to our exclusive measuring system, we forget that the rest of the natural world measures differently, and Mother Earth will eventually take action to maintain the stability of all subsystems in the biosphere.

We aren't that important — no single human being is — and the planet will be fine without us here. It bears repeating that in most cases this earth would actually be better off without our interference.

I mean, let's be real, humans cannot even connect that the species causing, without question, the most alterations to the earth in the history of time is somehow *not* responsible for the consequences that result from all that change.

That is textbook human behavior, and a special kind of stupid.

Nature absorbs the follies of humans, while we lack the resilience to survive the retaliation nature throws back our way.

We are fragile

We cannot handle nature's retaliation because we are fucking weak.

Pause.

Please take a few moments to finish beating your chest, rattling your sabers, and releasing your war cries. Wrap up all the other macho tough-guy shit you've been programmed to do in response to any challenge to our superiority, and emotionally regulate yourself so we can continue.

Our frailty is very obvious.

We are the most advanced species on the planet, yet somehow also the weakest in terms of unaided survival outside our *humanity bubble*.

Our technological prowess strengthens us in our *humanity bubble* but severely impedes our ability to function in the natural world. We've been on a very long journey to simplify our lives, and the results of our efforts render us incapable of surviving outside that artificial environment of ours that continues to engulf the planet voxel by voxel.

I gave in to the whole voxel thing. Sue me.

Despite the immense amount of resources that we dedicate to stalling the grim reaper, we are always one insect bite away from a very quick death when we step out into reality, and we are screwed if pollinators disappear from the planet.

And so, as our friendly neighborhood deer herd calmly looks on as their habitat is destroyed, puzzled by the anxious nature of the human herd feverishly assembling more data centers to tock and tick their lives away, these quadrupeds merely shrug it off and move to their next place of grazing, calling no specific piece of land their homes.

We, on the other hand, subconsciously pray that the power keeps flowing from that outlet as we continuously expand the nervous system of our *humanity bubble* — the electrical grid — onto the back of the rest of the earth, replacing the roots that nourish the natural world.

We're increasingly severing the natural connections as we substitute in our own system, effectively isolating ourselves from anything that could harm us. We're increasing our fragility as we inadvertently separate ourselves from what we need while building up the resilience of everyone else.

We fear the wild

Beyond our *humanity bubble* lies that great unknown.

The great outdoors.

The wild west.

Nature.

Nature is scary to us. Just think of the origins of the term *wild west*. Now more aligned with uncharted business environments, this term originally referred to that scary place heading west toward the Pacific, where people went to die of dysentery on that trail headed to Oregon.

The wild is not clean.

The wild is not temperature- or humidity-controlled.

The wild is not well lit — at least not until someone flicks a cigarette into the dry brush or installs some accent lighting.

The wild is everything our *humanity bubble* isn't.

We have been trained to run *into* the concrete jungle to chase our dreams, right into the living dream world that is our *humanity bubble*, but in reality we actually run *away* from what we need most.

Fresh air.

Clean drinking water.

Abundant basic foods.

For good measure, we'll also add silence to this list.

It truly is wild, the lengths we go to avoid the wild. See if you could sleep outside overnight with nothing. Hell, start by stepping outside into the darkness for 90 seconds.

No lights.

No protection.

Nothing.

Start there.

Turn off the air in the summer, or the heat in the winter.

Drink water right from a stream.

Eat something right from your yard that grew without direct human influence. I say once more that I am not a dietician and this next phrase is not dieting advice, but the evening primrose leaves that just simply grow in my yard are pretty tasty.

Humanity is on a quest to conquer the wild. To tame the environment around us and absorb it into our *humanity bubble*, replacing what we need most with those things we think we need.

Thankfully, the natural chaotic order of this world always returns.

We refuse to admit the limits

Our proclamation that we own the surface of this earth consequently establishes the requirement that land now serves our *humanity bubble*.

It must be productive for us. The land is now humanity's pantry.

Our hardware store.

Our resource emporium.

But how will we know when we grabbed the last cookie out of the jar?

With a few taps of my thumb, I can easily ascertain the exact product inventory in every store of a specific company across the planet, but how will we know when we are down to that last fish or last tree?

How about simply identifying the tipping point?

A lifetime of what we need always being on the shelves convinces us to errantly pass our flawed mindset to the next generation.

Forests as a high-level concept are renewable, but an individual tree won't necessarily grow back, depending on how it's removed and what is put in its place.

Nothing grows back if a building is there now.

Before realizing that I could simply raise the canopy on the last two trees in my backyard, I decided to cut them down. I did the research we all learn — getting multiple cost estimates for these services so I get the best monetary deal — but I certainly didn't go checking to make sure they weren't the last trees on the planet.

That's obvious.

What is not so obvious is the minimum number of trees we require on this planet to have enough oxygen for eight to nine *billion* of us to breathe, plus our other species friends.

I sure as hell don't know that number.

Nobody does.

Societally, we've never needed to know because the total tree population of earth has never been an issue in the *history of the planet*. Same goes for that fish population, or any other resource stock that we gleefully deplete as we skip along our unnatural path.

The earth has always been resource-abundant. Inventory has never mattered until we've recently decided the planet needed a substantial overhaul, and if you recall our two primary decision criteria from earlier for pursuing new endeavors — Does it make me money? Will I break the law? — we'll just keep firing away in the name of monetary gain so long as there are no rules or regulations in place to curtail our efforts.

Just because we can't find the line doesn't mean the line doesn't exist. It exists, and just because we have no formal legislation saying where the line is — and not to cross it — doesn't mean we should happily head in that direction.

If we cross that threshold we won't be able to just replant a tree.

We'll be dead, remember?

We can't live longer than about 5 minutes without the air they provide. At least we'll have those last breaths to collectively lament our poor life choices.

Those 50-year-old trees required 50 years to grow to their current maturity. That's a serious lag when compared to the half-day it takes for us to completely clear a few thousand square meters of trees, and I personally don't want to find out the hard way that we passed the critical point.

Citing insufficient data, we remain indifferent. Without regulatory guardrails, we remain convinced our actions are permissible. Returning to our unfettered access to all those products and services from before, we adopt a similar usage mindset — if we *shouldn't* do it, *someone* would stop us from doing it.

How do you collect high-fidelity data for something that can't be quantified?

Sales data makes sense, but we can't quantitatively represent the amount of trees you need in order to live.

How do you regulate something that can't truly be regulated?

I don't know, but why do we need a law in place to tell us to *not* make every free parcel of undeveloped land into a building?

Again, this should be obvious, since trees help you breathe. More trees is never a bad thing. Fewer trees is always bad.

By the time we could possibly legislate our way to ample legal protection for our essentials, we'll also be dead. We all see how the government works.

By the time we develop the computing power to provide supporting evidence for any legal proceedings on the matter, we'll also be dead because we will have cleared all the trees to build the computational firepower needed to crunch the numbers.

That would be on brand for us.

Clear the forests to put up data centers to tell us that we need a certain number of trees, and deploy legal stall tactics in the hellish labyrinth that is our judicial system while the natural world around us progressively falls.

Or.

Or we could just — stop cutting the trees down and allow equilibrium to return to the planet.

Just like our toothpaste or a bottle of shampoo, we use a resource liberally when we perceive the container is full — when we know there is plenty — but then as we approach the last few drops we suddenly start acting like we should have been from the beginning.

We ignore the fuel gauge and the recommended amounts that we truly need each time.

That's us.

That's our species.

That's what we do every day.

We simply cannot see how much is left. We are operating in the dark, and instead of tiptoeing cautiously, we close our eyes and charge forward, believing our invincibility will shield us even though we're about to smack right into a fucking wall.

Wasting when times are good, then finally conserving when we suddenly realize times are actually bad and we are forced to start rationing.

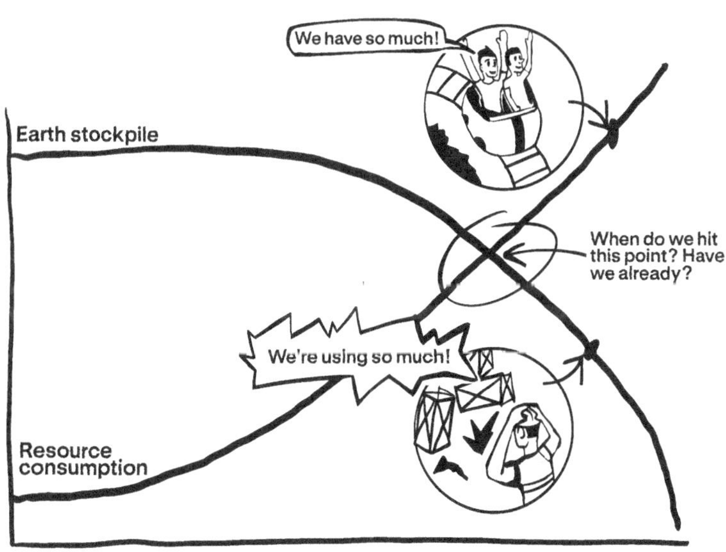

We are enjoying our ride to extinction

Everything we make takes us one step closer to doing less. Closer to using our bodies less, our five senses less, and our brains less.

I'd say we'll have the strongest fingers in the world from all our typing, but with voice-activated AI assistants and some other cutting-edge technology involving sensors implanted in our brains, it is possible we'll never again have to move a muscle to get what we want. We'll also never know what we want anymore, since once we connect our body's central computer to the *humanity bubble's* central computer, how would you truly know the data flow isn't bi-directional?

We're having a damn good time though and we don't really care about the long-term consequences.

We are clearly outpacing evolution but fail to realize in our haste that we took a hard left-turn and ended up on a different racetrack.

We are like the excited child who celebrates scoring in the wrong goal, except we ignorantly keep doing it for the remainder of the game, and into next season, and for the rest of our lives, despite very clear indications that it is wrong. All because there is nobody there to tell us otherwise and we are incapable of making the change on our own.

We are full speed ahead toward the precipice, but are forever convinced it's just a mirage and there truly is solid ground out there just beyond the cliff.

Even as we rush over the edge, we'll still manage to convince ourselves in those few zeptoseconds before gravity kicks in that there is solid ground below our feet.

Until we realize we are wrong and we plummet.

In our brains we expect the same subtle, incremental, snail-like pace on the way down that we experienced on our climb up.

An inexplicable and unjustifiable assumption of symmetry on the other side of the inflection point. The slow rise in the stock must be likewise matched by an easy ride back down the hill as we deplete that stock.

We expect a mirror image, but our behavior will cause a much different outcome. Once we reach that inflection point, we are in for a wild ride. No shortage of common metaphors exist for this situation, and you know them well.

Gradually pumping up the balloon or tire until it suddenly pops.

Slowly stretching the rubber band until it unexpectedly snaps.

Carefully bending the tree branch until it violently splinters.

Chaos ensues when things suddenly reverse course, which is amazing for nature, but bad news for our *humanity bubble*.

The 'fi' in sci-fi stands for fiction

It is quite unfortunate that the life we truly need to live would make for shitty television, because that little imagination box of ours seems to be where we derive our plans for the future.

Our endless sci-fi content paints a picture of the future we all seem to desire, but do you really want to live that type of life?

Or have we all just accepted our future of infinite growth and change and advancement as inevitable based on what we see in the movies?

Maybe it's a foregone conclusion that whatever we dream up in Sci-fi Land must eventually become reality with enough time and research.

The TV, our modern-day Oracle of Delphi.

Real life is boring and makes for bad ratings, so we spice it up a bit, then, forgetting TV isn't real, we emulate and consequently normalize in reality the behavior we see on those big screens.

Even that whole 'reality TV' thing isn't actually real, but that seemingly intuitive label alters our perception.

Would we have half the technology we have now if sci-fi didn't exist?

Who knows?

We could successfully defend both sides of the argument on whether reality drives our programming or vice versa, but in the end it's an irrelevant question since we don't *need* any of these gadgets in the first place.

Sci-fi is fictional — note the second half of that hyphenated abbreviation there — but nonetheless it somehow becomes our *non*-fictional roadmap.

Is that what we want?

Perhaps we can't seem to disrupt the tech frenzy because there is no alternative, and the only guiding light is what we see in the movies.

What's the equivalent vision for a different, more boring world, though? What if we could imagine a world that didn't involve all that technology, and just involved us merely existing in place?

Worst.

Movie.

Ever.

No shit, and that's the point. I don't want to watch that movie, I want to live it. Stop crossing the streams, and leave the imagination stuff in Imagination Land.

Go live out there in reality.

Delusions of interstellar domination

Back to our M^2 ambitions and our relentless quest to reach for the stars.

Colonizing another interstellar body presents a forced, unnatural intellectual challenge of epic proportions, while nurturing our current planet presents a natural emotional challenge.

Guess which one we flock toward? That's right, the hard one!

Deploy the engineering minds, all day every day, toward that holy grail of seemingly insurmountable engineering challenges!

The use of feminine pronouns to describe Mother Earth probably plays a role in our general species attitude toward not pursuing the latter option, but I can't really back that one up.

Leave it to us in all our *Homo sapiens* brilliance to decide in the course of about 75 years that we can create better living conditions with a clean slate on a new planet than we could if we simply restored harmony on the rock we're currently inhabiting. This planet of ours that quite naturally evolved over an inconceivably long amount of time to give us *exactly* what we need.

From "Houston, we have a problem" to "Hey, let's find another planet to live on and outbuild what we have on earth!" in less than a century.

Way to go.

We leverage the complexity of our work as an excuse to avoid our emotional shortcomings, and interstellar colonization represents the pinnacle intellectual challenge. An epically daunting problem behind which we can spend our entire lives hiding without being questioned, because the solution is unachievable in a single human lifetime.

I'm still not a psychologist, but one could claim the size of the intellectual challenge that an individual pursues is proportional to the amount of emotional dysregulation hidden deep within.

We avoid simple yet likely uncomfortable problems in everyday life by focusing on something so ridiculously unachievable, complex, and imaginary that we can effortlessly deem our actions unchallengeable.

How dare anyone question our motives as we work so hard on very important matters in the name of humanity.

Oblivious to the beautiful physical world around us as we dream of a future that we think will be 'more better' if we could just manufacture it ourselves.

Nevertheless, bon voyage to those that wish to depart. We'll be sure to pack some of those elusive and abstract thoughts and prayers for your trip.

Good job, guys.

Yes.

Guys.

Us men and our imbalances. Our confounding sense that we constantly have something to prove while also insisting we need to hide from a solid two-thirds of the emotional spectrum to maintain our toughness.

Solving the intellectual challenge of getting to an interstellar body is valued greater than the inward reflection of asking how we can nurture the planet we already occupy back to health.

Maybe we are deliberately emulating our clever water supply approach and destroying the planet so badly that we suddenly have no choice but to pursue the baffling and inexplicably more cost-effective option of heading into space to find a new home.

That's been a recurring theme for us, so please spare the masses all this pain and suffering and just go do the actual difficult work of re-integrating with this vast, beautiful world we already occupy.

Stop trying to go to space.

We are right where we need to be, and last time I checked, that whole colonization thing didn't go so well on this planet, so let's not scale that clusterfuck of a game plan up to the galactic level.

Just go take a day off.

Leave work a little early.

Catch your kid's ballgame, match, meet, play, spelling bee, or recital.

Stop trying to singlehandedly save the world.

Stop spending months writing a silly book that insults all of humanity in the hope that it'll singlehandedly save the world.

I'm back with more self-awareness!

I would prefer to avoid having my great[10]-granddaughter write a follow-up to this book that reports we were the only species to destroy a perfectly good planet we already inhabited that evolved to our unique needs, in order to create the technology necessary to travel some 200 million kilometers to stick a flag on the surface of another planet just to say we did it.

Tell you what — you want to go live on another interstellar body?

Awesome, but first please step outside our *humanity bubble* and survive a month in the wild before forcing us to endure your delusional master plans.

Leave all your fucking gadgets at home.

Unless we start [thinking about]...

Alright, the tension is building a bit, so everyone just put down the electronics for a moment and CTFO.

Chill The Fuck Out.

We've lost our humanity behind our keyboards and our cameras as we spray grotesque invective with reckless abandon across the globe with the casual click of a button.

Our brains have been hijacked, so it's time for a reset. A great first step would be to return from this dream world within a dream world that is the internet and at least recalibrate to physically being in our *humanity bubble* again. Get out of the virtual rabbit holes you're all climbing down and take a breath.

Despite my insistence throughout this book that we suck as a species, I'm still rooting for us. Our species is like my home state. I hate us, but I love us, so in the end I have hope.

Somewhere along our species timeline we simply deviated off course. We fell out of sync with other species, convinced we could remake the world without consequence to suit our personal wants. Persuaded into thinking this real life game where we simulate a city doesn't actually affect anything.

This decision gradually evolved over time — a *long* period of time — meaning it won't be solved in a day, nor should we try to be that quick about it.

I already asked multiple times throughout this book for you to not make any behavioral challenges in defense of my retirement portfolio, but there are a few ways to accomplish that little head-tilt we talked about earlier. That subtle reorientation that us humans in this present moment are responsible for initiating to reset our course.

As a reminder, the assignment is not necessarily to *do* anything listed here. Just simply *think* about a few of these things.

That's it.

Pick one or two that resonate with you and give them some thought. There are only seven of them, a nice prime number for everyone.

They aren't quite orders, laws, canons, or edicts. I'd go with commitments but that's probably too triggering given its similarity to another c-o-m-m- word — no commanding happening here — so we'll just call them the seven contemplations.

Choose whatever label you wish, just consider them carefully.

Re-integrating with the natural world

Our *humanity bubble* is isolated from the rest of the planet, and it is time to reestablish harmony with the other systems on this rock.

It is also time to re-evaluate our relationships with all of our *non-human* neighbors.

We all have a little 'wild' in us, and I pity those who refuse to embrace this part of themselves and relentlessly suppress it to save face in our *humanity bubble*, in the name of preserving some unspoken divine innocence that none of us could truly articulate if asked.

Fuck that. Embrace your wild within.

Preferably not in a way that invites anarchy or damage to others, though. There is no need for a purge, but we can head in the other direction a bit since a few millennia of domestication will not so easily overwrite myriad millennia of instinct.

I love being human.

We are amazing creatures, but that's all we are.

Creatures.

We believe we can perpetually pursue solutions to all these self-generated non-problems, but regardless of what we tell ourselves, we will at some point snap back to balance.

Back to the anchor point.

When you're the only *human* doing something incredible and unorthodox in the office, you're a trailblazer, but when you're the only *species* doing something equally unique, the species in question should probably evaluate their life choices. They are the weird ones, the ones out of line, so consider doing a little something every day that pushes you toward reintegrating with the natural world.

It doesn't have to be big. Seriously, just keep it simple.

Spend more time outside.

Stand barefoot on the grass for 20 seconds.

Move more.

Grow more of your own food.

Don't squash that spider.

Let your yard grow unabated.

Go somewhere where you can truly experience nature's impact. We don't belong boxed up in these containment bubbles we've created for ourselves, isolated from everything else in the world.

Baby steps. That's all you need to do.

On the off chance that there are a few 'go big or go home' types out there with a bunch of extra credits you don't know how to use, buy a lot in a downtown metropolitan area, remove all signs of human modification from it, and leave it barren for the next forever.

No takers? No worries, I'll try eventually.

Embracing community

It is also time to reconnect with our *human* neighbors.

Skip your social media circles and build quality relationships out there in reality with people in your immediate physical surroundings.

Go meet your neighbors.

If you see them outside or pass them on the street, say hello and strike up a genuine human-to-human conversation.

No phones.

You don't have to instantly become besties, and don't fucking dare ask who they voted for.

Just ask how they're doing. A sincere "How are you?" or "What's happening with you?" is a severely underused gateway to intimate connection.

Revisit the definition of *intimate* on your own before you freak out on me because you think I want you to date your neighbors.

Remember that your best friend should be another human.

In fact, find a few.

There are amazing and lonely people out there anxiously awaiting the cathartic experience of human interaction. So, before you attempt shoving your peacock on a plane in the name of emotional support — it happened, look it up — maybe just pause, stop taking the easy way out by forcing affection on a lesser being, and work through the awkwardness of interacting with our own kind to establish strong, lasting connections.

Establish common ground through certain communities, but don't stay there.

Find your differences.

Celebrate them.

Discuss them.

Debate them.

Don't default to anger when you disagree with them, and I'll stress once more the importance of embracing awkwardness. It's weird for everyone, so just push through.

Be human.

Smile.

Laugh a bit.

Laugh at yourself when you slip up.

Avoid the path into silence or anger. Make those mistakes.

We all do it. Forgive yourself and press on.

Be curious, not combative.

Passersby may look scary staring down intently at their phones, but the warmth they exude once they look up in response to you saying hello as you pull them back to reality is worth it.

Feel that warmth. Feel life flow through you.

Pull them from the throes of their imaginary world and kindly bring them into reality.

Every one of us is subconsciously hoping someone will say hello.

Be the initiator.

Take the leap.

Just don't go walking down the street in the city saying hello to every single person you pass.

That's weird. Use your judgment and find the right balance.

Stripped of the opportunity to randomly interact with neighbors and friends at the local general store, or to talk with the shop owner, we must create those scenarios ourselves.

All those stores are disappearing, and every single thing we need magically shows up on our doorstep, stealthily dropped off by that new army of delivery ninjas, the only evidence of their presence being the package on the doorstep and a picture of your porch now saved on a stranger's phone that they send you to verify delivery.

I still remember my delivery driver Pete from childhood.

Same guy, same route, every time.

Empathizing with all species

The word *empathy* is a pain in the ass. Everyone has an interpretation, so of course I happily present mine here, with the caveat that my empathy expands beyond the human species to other living creatures.

The rabbit that I scared out of my front garden earlier today is just as much a part of my community as my human neighbors. To be honest, I like my rabbit friends more than some of the humans walking the earth right now, and I really felt bad for startling it while it was searching for a meal.

I still lament the pair of birds I killed with my car as they landed in the middle of the road when I came speeding through, admittedly in a rush to go nowhere fast.

I remember the chipmunk I ran over entering my neighborhood over a decade ago, and I can still hear and feel the 'thump' of contact as life left its body. I just gave myself chills from simply writing about it.

I felt like an asshole the other day when I started closing my patio umbrella and crushed the antenna and front legs of a young cricket. Yes, a cricket! I unsurprisingly found it dead on the table the next day, and I reflected on my carelessness as I absolutely buried that poor corpse in my compost pile.

I still feel the pop reverberating through my hand and arm when I crushed a cockroach the other day. Yes, it was in the house. No, I don't care.

I shed a tear when I see roadkill, praying for the raccoon, deer, or opossum as its lifeless body lies there, motionless and mangled. I shed that tear in the same way I do when witnessing unfair treatment of helpless humans by those who should know better.

I've come to terms with my newfound emotional activation and outright dismiss any claims it demonstrates weakness. Hatred and apathy are easy, as evidenced by how they spread like wildfire.

Fiercely advocating for those that are inferior to you takes a backbone.

Empathy is actually easier to understand when relating it to other species. This emotional concept, in my eyes, has nothing to do with presumably knowing what it feels like to actually *be* another human or animal.

That's an idiotic premise.

What we *can* do is imagine a relatable experience to help understand what that other living being — human or otherwise — *might* be feeling, and use that insight as a moral compass to guide our behavior.

For example, we can't imagine how it would feel to be a bug as a human steps on us, but I'm sure most of us could simply liken the experience to how it would feel being instantly crushed in a trash compactor, and reasonably conclude that's a shitty day that we shouldn't impose on others.

We've seen enough crazy sci-fi movies and horror films showing humans navigating dangerous, downright demented, and potentially fatal escape rooms and obstacle courses to scare the shit out of us. We should also be able to relate that imagined experience to what it might be like for other species to navigate around all our *humanity bubble* nonsense. Pathways with fast-moving projectiles. Large machines that can destroy an animal's home in seconds. A dominant, allegedly non-invasive species that could unpredictably cuddle you or kill you on a whim. Fences, walls, partitions, dams, nets, domes.

In theory that *should* be enough of a connection to think twice about indiscriminately harming other living things out of fear or boredom, or treating others poorly as we translate the premise back to the human level.

In theory.

That's my take.

Define this weaponized word any way you wish, just be a decent human.

Adulting the right way

Technically we are all adults by 18 or 21 years old, and we learn a lot of great skills along the way.

Talking, crawling, walking, looking before crossing the street, saving for retirement, cooking our own food, wiping ourselves, building things, speaking publicly.

All great stuff.

But a funny thing happens as the majority of us become adults. We go from hearing we can't get *every*thing we want to hearing we can have *any*thing we want if we are willing to work for it or have the money to pay for it.

It's one of the major child-to-adult transitions that goes in the wrong direction.

We are left with the impression that once we arrive in adulthood the shackles fall off and we can achieve whatever we wish if we just put our minds to it, which I initially agreed with until I realized what it's doing to us on a systemic level. Our little consciousness cricket normally on our shoulders has apparently called in sick, and we take that opportunity to smash our own moral compasses in our transition from adolescence.

No higher power keeps us in line as we proceed to run amok.

It's like we were held back for so long during childhood that we explode onto the scene as we cross the adulthood mark, aggressively seeking the things we want because we feel we deserve them while ignoring the resources required to obtain them.

We may meet the legal age requirement to be considered an adult, but do we meet the behavioral requirements?

We want it all.

We can't have it all.

I so badly want to say we can't have our cake and eat it too, but I'm not going to do it because I've exhausted my cliché allotment.

We are not that special, and resources are *not* infinite, yet we insist otherwise with our entitled behavior that reinforces our narrative that we can act with impunity.

We can choose to keep acting this way — freedom and whatnot — but our broken gauge says the resource tank is full when it's really bone dry, and we're just squeezing out the residual remains of what's left in the pipes right now.

Programmed from childhood to want things we can't have and to achieve record-setting greatness in various games, we take that same mentality to adulthood to drive up the high score in a new game — the mature and respectable game of growing your personal net worth — while simultaneously removing any ceilings in our way as we cross into full maturity.

Our childhood environment promotes an unhealthy desire for toys at an early age, serving as a mere training ground for us to eventually demand more expensive and resource-intensive dopamine-releasing toys in adulthood.

We stand alone in terms of altering the face of this world.

Those actions have an impact.

That impact is not always immediate.

That impact may occur elsewhere, or even at a different time.

We're still responsible, even if the consequence presents itself later, in ways you wouldn't expect, in places you've never been.

I kick a classmate on the playground, I get detention.

I drop a glass dish, it breaks.

I drop that glass dish on my bare foot, and my body lets me know immediately how badly that hurt.

I run a red light, I get pulled over.

I haphazardly replace an electrical outlet without turning off the power, I get zapped.

I leave the car windows open and it rains, the interior gets soaked.

These examples are the typical action-reaction pairs we know well, where obviously connected, direct, and immediate outcomes happen in pretty much the same place.

It's very easy for our brains to take the shortcut to believing 'no harm, no foul' when we don't see this relationship, but we have a responsibility to do better.

To be better.

Better to ourselves.

Better to our neighbors of all species.

Better with the *finite* resources we have available to us.

If we can't accept that role, then we deserve our fate, which at this rate is — that's right — see that book title once more!

Self-extinction, or something like that.

Heavy is the crown.

I went a page or two before I "cliché'd" again. Almost made it.

We can no longer act like annoying kids in the damn candy store, uncontrollably indulging without paying any attention to the impact our gluttony has on our surroundings.

True freedom is dangerous without self-discipline and personal accountability.

If you act responsibly, you don't need guardrails. If you don't want guardrails, then start acting responsibly.

It amazes me with all those fucking mirrors everywhere that we still fail to clearly see that elusive 'someone' that can very easily guide us in the right direction.

That 'someone' is ourselves.

Doing a bit less sometimes

Do less. *Less* doesn't necessarily mean *none*, and *do* doesn't mean *do forever*. There is an entire multi-axis spectrum to consider, so don't jump to the extremes, and don't be so binary about it. It's not all black and white, so please turn that dial down from 11.

Don't think in terms of being a daily couch potato or a marathoner.

Daily latte, or no lattes ever.

Bike everywhere, or drive everywhere.

Meat daily, or meat never.

Learn to embrace the gray area without feeling obligated to maintain a *permanent* happy medium. Think like this:

Take a walk one day a week after work for a month.

Skip a latte on the weekends for a few weeks.

Bike to work twice a month during the summer.

Whatever your normal protein choice, try the other one this winter.

Also, the other end of the spectrum isn't by default your enemy, so take a deep breath and drop your guard a bit.

Keeping it simple

We expend an overwhelming majority of our creativity on getting around barriers we put in our own way, and we fail to acknowledge that one viable solution to these barriers when they arise is to do less of the thing that caused them in the first place.

The result is a complex web of preposterous systems we all just presume is normal. Here are a few places where we cling to a complex system when a simple one would do.

We maintain absurd systems like this fucking food system of ours, where it truly is a wonder that we are all still alive.

We exhaust ourselves for half a century in our prime years to earn the right to finally rest, then delay death as long as possible to hopefully enjoy 20 years of life well after our natural human expiration date.

We painstakingly create transportation systems where we are awarded the opportunity to be productive in traffic instead of finding ways to just not be in traffic.

We stopped working our muscles through natural movement and substituted in a complex and arbitrary exercise regimen.

Why are there no quiet toilets? No idea, but we wouldn't need one — or any of our fancy waste-related innovations — if we all just went right on the ground or in the water like normal animals.

While we're on the topic of acting like normal animals, let's all die a little more simply too. Just make sure we're embracing that whole quality over quantity mentality with our years first.

We seem inexplicably entranced with destroying a planet that forever evolved to effortlessly provide us with what we need, in order to relocate to a planet where we have nothing so we can prove our ability to persevere, when we couldn't last a minute in the wilderness that exists right outside our city limits.

We keep generating more electricity instead of just using less, constantly defying Jevon at every turn.

And finally — 70,000+ pages dictating collection of tax revenue?

Really?

Embrace simple living.

Straddling the fence

I am not advocating for indecisiveness with this title, but instead suggesting that it is possible to consider and evaluate two sides of a discussion objectively without your entire world collapsing.

You can do it. It will be okay.

Translating that idea to our current subject, you can promote an idea for the future while still functioning normally in the present reality in which we find ourselves.

It's not hypocritical. It's actually quite sensible, and any other mindset would cause paralysis. Transitions take time. Candles didn't vanish the moment Edison flipped the switch on the first light bulb.

You don't need to cling to the old way on Tuesday and then hastily apply the new and better way on Wednesday when it is first revealed.

Embrace and consider contradictory stances, acknowledging that your feet can be on different sides of a [hopefully very low] fence. That's why you will still find me doing most things I passionately critiqued in this book.

I truly wish to slow down, but I'm still pushing the limits every day.

I don't want to work, but I still get in a car and commute every day. That's right, I ended up back at work.

'Process improvement' appears in my new job description multiple times despite my advocacy for a simple life and criticism of humanity for constantly seeking a better way. It pays today's bills.

I still reluctantly stare at a computer because it also pays the bills.

I re-wild my backyard hoping one day that it could sustain me, but still use the grocery store because I would starve otherwise. The transition is in progress, and since my neighbors are not following suit, it only makes sense that critters will flock to my yard to eat, severely delaying my self-sufficient living.

I accept my constant relapses into sugar-fueled snacking despite my promoting a very basic and healthy diet.

Returning to a system of free food and free water is a great idea, but a stupid one to implement in our current system because someone will collect all the free stuff and sell it.

I want everyone to stop buying stupid shit, but I let it go because of that retirement portfolio I nagged you about constantly.

I spent more than enough pages in this book bashing an industry I've spent my career working in, but know full well that throwing down your weapons in this present day is a death sentence. At the end of the day, we haven't really been talking out our problems all that long. Our species has spent thousands of years smashing each other's heads in with a rock to settle our differences, and up until a few centuries ago, gentlemen were still dueling to settle their differences.

I keep picking up the weights and putting them down for now, until I can adopt a lifestyle that doesn't require it.

I think there are too many humans roaming the earth, but long-term natural attrition is a perfectly acceptable solution. No need for sinister plans to infect half the world with a deadly virus to abruptly course-correct our population numbers.

Sorry, I just watched a crazy action movie with a similar plot. Yes, I still watch sci-fi movies despite my desire to live naturally.

I still shave my head every Sunday, and look at myself in every damn reflective surface that I pass.

I still love pets. I just cuddled a cat right now and it was marvelous. Reconsider that whole animal ownership thing later, but not right now if you have them already. Getting rid of the ones you have now would be downright cruel, but maybe skip the whole 'own another creature' thing the next time around.

Keep going out, doing the things, and maintaining your traditions, but don't remain there if you wish life to be different.

Thank you for enduring what should have just been an inner monologue reconciling where I am and where I want to be.

Closing statements

I now lay to rest my outrageous condemnation of humanity. Congrats on sticking it out until the end, and if I did my job right I successfully managed to piss off all demographics equally.

Let's quickly repeat that painfully academic thesis as we close out this most excellent of adventures. I think you're supposed to repeat it in the conclusion, right? I'll never figure this whole writing thing out, but at any rate, here it is:

Our continuous isolation from the biosphere and our significant imbalance with nature will eventually lead us to self-extinction. As we partition ourselves from the rest of the system, we refuse to acknowledge the detrimental effects of our actions out of view beyond our immediate surroundings. We are pushing out of balance with the natural world because we have a false sense of abundance, we are obsessed with comfort, and contentment continues to elude us.

The comfortable but artificial world we built removed the need for us to solve our most basic species-level problems.

Where should we sleep?

Where can we find clean water?

How will we find food today?

How will we stay safe?

No longer burdened with the requirement to secure our true needs, our idle minds aimlessly meander through humanity's playground in search of innovation, improvement, and advancement opportunities as a means of staying occupied. We now face a presumably more pressing set of questions.

How can we stay busy?

What should we solve?

How can we remain intellectually stimulated?

Can we do something in a better way?

How can we make more money?

We gradually mislabeled wants as needs on our wild species journey, leading us to errantly desire things our ancestors couldn't fathom.

Imagine handing Alexander Graham Bell a modern-day cell phone, Henry Ford a supercar, or Alan Turing a computer with AI. Could you even fathom Lewis & Clark with a Satnav?

"You mean it just *shows* you the exact route? It tracks how long it'll take you to get there? It reroutes you if there's an obstacle?"

These innovations greatly improved modern life, but they drastically altered what it means to live. As animals we don't need any of it, but we refuse to give any of it up.

We choose not to.

We could change course at any time. There is nothing that says we must continue on this materialistic path.

We just choose not to.

We reinforce these choices by teaching our youth skills that emphasize advancement in our *humanity bubble* at the expense of survival outside of it.

Our societal conformity leaves us woefully unprepared at the individual level for survival in nature, where every other species on the planet resides, and our poor planning is clearly evident when the natural world penetrates our fabricated living space.

While we waste our time pursuing meaningless achievements, Mother Nature patiently bides her time and carries on as always.

See the systems at play

You thought you were done with all the systems stuff, didn't you?

Think again!

I will interject the annoyingly complex stuff one last time to further highlight the intricacies of the systems we deal with daily. We'll pile onto the complexity with two last facets I left out up front.

Systems constantly shift over time

Systems are dynamic. Pretend you open the front door to a cat lady's apartment, and someone gave all 73 of her felines some catnip and their very own yarn ball with a unique color. The inevitable dense web of multi-colored yarn crossing the room basically conveys the complicated connections in these systems.

Oh, and by the way, the cats keep moving and changing the string paths as you look on in horror, and also the whole apartment building looks like this, with each dwelling having its own century of cats. In fact, the entire block is set up this way, and the cats keep escaping and swapping buildings as they bring their yarn along.

Meanwhile, our *humanity bubble* is a mere speck of dust on one of those yarn strands, going along on a wild ride.

Systems have many layers

The *humanity bubble* itself contains additional subsystem layers. In the same way we create our own personal comfort zone around us as individuals — a topic worthy of its own book that I'll get to if this one works out — we likewise create multiple concentric bubbles within our world.

Let's hit a few highlights from top to bottom.

Our species bubble. That *humanity bubble* I've referenced throughout this book.

Our country bubble. Try again to show up to a border crossing without claiming to be from a specific country. At least one country claims ownership over each of us.

Our regional/state/provincial bubble. Any one of these three entities in between a country and community.

Our community bubble. Those in our immediate surroundings (150 or so people). Our tribe.

Our family bubble. Doesn't have to be blood, by the way. Family is whatever you make it, and looks any way you want it to look.

Our individual bubble. Who we are as individuals. Beautiful, amazing, and unique beings that all bring something to the table, especially when we find an environment where we can truly and safely be ourselves.

Six layers of systems. Or subsystems?

Russian nesting dolls, except each doll has a way to interlock with others, and we can unite through any one of these common threads.

Keep peeling back the onion and you can find a bubble of sorts for any of the endless groups within that community level, one in which we find our people and hide in the comfort of like-minded ideals.

Writers.

Crocheters.

Religious types.

Gardeners.

Bonsai enthusiasts.

Veterans.

Chefs.

Political party people.

Dancers.

Socialites.

Firearm owners.

Painters.

Influencers.

Card collectors.

Celebrities.

Sports people.

People will guard their territory quite ferociously, too. Let's look at that last one: sports.

- Stop off in Boston and loudly proclaim your love for a specific set of pinstripes.

- Stroll down the streets of Philly with your big blue cap on and see how it goes for you. Hell, proclaim your love for the birds and you'll probably experience the same reaction, knowing how that city rolls.

- Profess your love for a 'real' football club in Madrid while in Barcelona.

- Head into Ohio wearing a big gold 'M' on your shirt.

I can't help but mention the two north-eastern bullets leading off this section, a regional bubble.

We should come together around anything that piques our interest, but the groups we find should not become our entire world. Use the bubble as common ground to navigate the awkwardness of a new social interaction, but it should not become our identity. Camaraderie with fellow bubble-mates cannot lead to uniting against perceived outsiders.

Accept the other bubbles out there.

Accept them not because of some unwritten obligation to agree across the board, but because of their right to exist as an entity. Grab a cup of coffee with someone from one of those other ostracized bubbles. People have great depth, and it's likely that there's a vibrant, good-natured human in there somewhere.

Those people and their bubbles are not our enemies.

I am bookending our discussion with more systems stuff because it sheds light on how 'not easy' this all is.

There is no panacea for what ails us, and anyone selling an easy, quick fix is hoodwinking the masses for their own gain.

Reevaluate those stupid questions

We hit a lot of stupid questions in this book, and while I could probably fill a few more pages with every single one of them, here is the highlight reel:

- How the hell are we still here?

- What makes us so uniquely equipped to run the show on this planet?

- What does *a long time* really mean?

- Who is the *'they'* that keeps all these norms of ours in place?

- What exactly is that *'system'* that we claim is broken?

- What does *'clean'* actually mean?

- What if those lazy felines are the ones doing life right?

- Would stagnation be such a bad thing?

- Why should we care how our actions affect the distant future?

- What would *enough* feel like?

- What is a true problem?

- How would we fare if we had to fend for ourselves with nothing but our bare hands?

- How the hell are we all somehow on defense?

- Why do we choose plants that satisfy our eyes and not satiate our stomachs?

- Isn't it odd that we have to so arduously maintain the supposedly natural part of our property?

- If what's in our vegetable gardens is so valuable that we need to heavily fortify the perimeter, why do we dedicate such a small percentage of our property to that purpose?

- Why can't we just have free food and water everywhere?

- Why is land where we bury our dead considered off-limits and untouchable in perpetuity?

- Why do dead people have addresses?

- What do we actually need all that electricity for anyway?

- What natural, biological processes are we disrupting by blocking other species from accessing the water directly from the land?

- Does anyone else remember ceding ownership of themselves — our precious *citizenship* — to an abstract organizational entity?

- Are we honestly comfortable entrusting such a complex food system, one over which we have no control, with providing us the essentials we need to live?

- Why are we downright careless with resources so critical to our survival?

- Can we confidently guarantee for ourselves and our loved ones that our essentials will always be there?

- What would we do if those essentials weren't there one day?

- Isn't it concerning that the essentials we need to survive aren't readily available? Wouldn't we want those essentials to be abundant?

- Does the direction we are heading with potable water filtration requirements seem sensible given our inability to live a day or two without it?

- Did anyone ask those oxen if they were okay with working for us against their will?

- What genius had the brilliant idea to tightly restrain another living creature around the fucking neck?

- What other species besides humans requires such ginger handling?

- What purpose does owning a pet serve?

- Our pets can survive without us, but can we survive without them?

- How is hanging a dead carcass on the wall aesthetically appealing?

- Why does a monkey need to play computer games?

- Do humans meet the requirements of an invasive species?

- If the chemicals we apply to the ground require us to prevent animals from being on it, should we really be putting it on the ground to begin with?

- If we could query every other species on this planet, how would they say things are going?

- Why have we accepted a system that prevents us from slowing down during the months when our essentials are sparse?

- Why are rainy days bad?

- Why does the land meant to feed humans need to create wacky marketing gimmicks just to stay in business?

- Why do you want to be strong?

- Would we have ever thought of being on a phone in the bathroom 50 years ago?

- Is anyone else still wondering why this bald guy was at a hair salon?

- What's your personal lifetime resource consumption so far?

- Why do we so fervently support pulling humans from poverty, this strictly economic measure that is meaningless outside our *humanity bubble* construct?

- Why does that support suddenly end once we've collectively reached the middle?

- Has anyone ever seen another species organizing a funeral?

- Do we all really desire the picturesque life sci-fi paints for us?

- We may meet the age requirement to be considered an adult, but do we meet the behavioral requirements?

- What's the right type of abundance?

To close I'll ask one last stupid question: How far did you make it down this list before you felt like an idiot?

Keep pushing through.

Read them out loud.

Say them to others.

Ask your own stupid questions too.

Don't dismiss them as obvious, and don't let others brush them aside.

Challenge yourself.

Challenge others.

If you can't get past thinking of these as stupid questions, then instead consider them as a way to challenge our norms, because as the superior member of the animal kingdom we do a lot of stupid shit.

Ponder these perspectives

We've collectively sullied the good name of terms like *truth* and *facts*, so I will refrain from using those exact words. I will merely acknowledge upfront that the one truth I can say with absolute certainty is that I truly don't know a fucking thing.

Neither do you.

It's all perspective, and with that, I present my perspectives for your reading pleasure as we wrap things up:

- We are the only species that refuses to slow down.

- We are the only species manipulating the elements to create things.

- We are the only species deliberately splitting atoms.

- I don't see anyone else out there lighting up a fire to cook their caribou out on the savannah.

- We claimed ownership over the land meant for all species using language on legal documents created by humans that only humans understand.

- We cede most life decisions to similar legal documents — contracts, we call them — by making our mark next to a lot of confusing words.

- Land is expensive for the wrong reasons.

- Nature requires loose, moist soil. Our *humanity bubble* requires dry, compacted soil.

- Nature doesn't invade. Nature reclaims. Nature grows. Anything we create in our *humanity bubble* decays.

- We allow land ownership to continue into death.

- No other species has altered the face of this earth in the way we have.

- Our nuclear power plant revival of the 2020s came about solely because we wanted more computing power.

- We don't know what starving means.

- We are the only species adamantly demanding that every land-water boundary on the face of the planet is forever fixed in place.

- Legal, ethical, just, moral. One of these is not always righteous.

- We are the only species with landfills. We are the only species with stuff that gets dumped in those landfills.

- We consciously breed species as the foundation of our food supply.

- That castrated bull is pretty damn strong despite only eating grass.

- Our plates can have chicken. Our plates can have tofu. Our plates can have both chicken and tofu right next to each other.

- We have an inexplicable compulsion to own living creatures, even humans.

- We are afraid to test our crazy creations on ourselves first.

- There are too many of us.

- There is a multi-year gap between when the human body biologically indicates when it can start reproducing, and when humans culturally indicate it is time to start reproducing.

- We have driven at least one other species to extinction.

- Poachers don't poach eggs.

- No other species checks the time.

- No other species intentionally awakens to an alarm clock.

- The greater the desire for growth, the greater the discontent.

- Salad can be a delicious breakfast.

- We are the only species that discovered a way to drink joules.

- We are the only species indulging in dessert, and oddly enough the only species voluntarily living in the desert.

- Thirst comes first.

- We are the only species that invented something in which we deposit our waste.

- No other species voluntarily sticks needles in their face to look good.

- Our reproduction now depends on the electrical grid.

- Without the comforts of our *humanity bubble*, the human life span is still two to four decades.

- Only a human could possibly contemplate immortality.

- Extra years are no substitute for fewer years lived well.

- Technology is optional.

- No one could know how it feels to be a deer. Just think of what it would be like to run blindfolded across a freeway.

- We are the only species competing against Mother Nature in a 'we can do it better' competition.

- Sorry, you're not a winner. That's okay, though, because life isn't a game to be played.

We're at the home stretch here folks, almost done!

- We pursue knowledge instead of pursuing our essentials. We protect our data more vigilantly than we protect those essentials.

- With all of those sensors and dashboards and diagnostics powered by our amazing computing machines, we no longer have a need for those naturally endowed five senses of ours.

- Despite its awkwardness, myriad can in fact be used as an exact number (10,000) and not just as abstract hyperbole. I think I even used century somewhere to denote *100*.

- You are probably wrong. It's okay.

- Mind your words. As an unverified descendant of one of those two dictionary people, I implore us all to understand the meaning of the words coming out of our mouths. In the same way you can't sing with conviction unless you truly know the lyrics, you cannot speak wisely when lacking any knowledge or understanding of what your words mean.

- Oh, and sing more. Just make sure you know the words first.

Lastly, and quite randomly, we are the only species that grows a specific species of tree for the sole purpose of severing them from their nutrient source, propping them up in our living rooms for a few weeks, and decorating them for a holiday celebration.

Humbug — and to all a good night.

Side with nature

Millennia from now I hope someone asks the same question I posed at the start:

"How the hell are we still here?"

My hope, though, is that they ask that same question from the perspective of being shocked that humans actually fucking did it. That we successfully tilted our heads a bit and subtly changed our ways just enough in the early 21st century to open the door for future generations to harmoniously thrive with the rest of the natural world.

Am I being overly optimistic?

Damn right I am. We need positivity right now.

I am hopeful, but not because I am expecting big things out of us as a species. Quite the opposite, actually, as our job couldn't be any easier.

I am hopeful because our specific responsibility, at the time of this writing, is not big at all. It's so freaking simple anyone could do it. I'm no neurologist, but I'm thinking just a handful of neurons should be enough to handle the task.

Simple, easy, basic, and painless micro-adjustments. That one-degree shift in our trajectory today to make sure we end up in the right place 15,348 years from now. We must be the start of the exponential curve, implementing minimal change that produces unmeasurable results now but forms the foundation for immense change later.

While we are humans, a species, we are also a collective of individual be-ings who get to make decisions for themselves, and so we just need a few of us to lead the way.

An emboldened group of us making subtle changes in how we interact with the world.

Small changes in how we interact with our fellow species.

And most importantly, small changes amongst ourselves.

Our present troubles aren't the fault of human beings walking the earth today.

The past is not on us, but what happens next is.

I've made my choice. I'm with the natural world.

It's time to make yours.

Who is this guy, anyway?

We've established throughout this book that I have relinquished my title as an engineer, and I am also not an expert, a prompt engineer, an earth-whisperer, a psychologist, an economist, a dietician, a dog-whisperer, a pharmaceutical scientist, a business major, an anatomist, a singer, or a neurologist.

As this is my first written work, the jury is still out on whether the title of writer can apply.

I am just another human, one with lofty dreams of a world where I can step outside to grab all I need to survive. A world where asphalt and concrete are nowhere to be seen, and shoes, chairs, and desks are no longer needed. A world that successfully prioritizes the right type of abundance.

I spent the first half of my professional career tackling complex technical problems, and now I am focusing on the more important problem of how to live a simple, more fulfilling life in my second act.

I aim for a different type of high score now: seeing how many hectares of land I can protect from egregious human influence.

I am a citizen of earth, and despite the allure of interstellar travel and an engineering background incessantly nagging me to find a way into space — and a strange habit where everything I build with blocks eventually becomes a spaceship — I plan to spend my time on this planet healing our one true home, until it comes time for the earth to absorb my body.

I dream of a world I know I will never see, but happily live my humble, minimalist life in the hope that humanity gets there. I truly believe we can reshape this world, and that transformation starts with us in this moment.

Don't let the excessive use of em-dashes fool you. This work is my own. I wrote that way before the computer overlords hijacked a perfectly reasonable, acceptable, and functional punctuation mark — these things — to (a) indicate a pause or emphasis in a sentence, (b) introduce an explanation, or (c) mark a sudden break or change in thought.

Despite my recent exploration into eclectic musical genres, I remain a life-long metalhead, and I playfully dropped a few dozen subtle references to some of my favorite hard rock bands throughout this book.

48, to be exact. If you're up for a scavenger hunt, let us all know on the socials which ones you find.

Say what you wish about those raucous mosh pits full of intense and explosive energy, but if the person next to you goes down at any time, for any reason, the group pauses and creates a space around the fallen.

Sometimes you lend a hand, sometimes you just keep the space clear for them to rise again on their own. Either way, the crowd creates an environment where all have the chance to safely find their own way back to their feet at their own pace.

Lastly, those lottery numbers I promised you: 1,2,3,4,5. Better go change your luggage combination.

Be bold. Stand tall. Kill with kindness.

Brian

Written in this most insane of years, 2025